The Blood Tattoo

Third Edition

by Ebi Gabor

Monument Press   Memphis, TN

The Blood Tattoo
Copyright ©1997, 2006 by Ebi Gabor

ISBN-10: 0-9748463-3-3
ISBN-13: 978-0-974846-33-0
Formerly published as ISBN: 0-930383-11-7

All rights reserved. Printed in the United States of America. No part of this book may be reproduced in any manner whatsoever without written permission except in the case of brief quotations embodied in critical articles and reviews. For information, contact the publisher.

Cover photo of Ebi Gabor © Photography With Heart 06, D. F, Wente

Cover photo courtesy of The United States Holocaust Memorial Museum:
"THE VIEWS OR OPINIONS EXPRESSED IN THIS BOOK, AND THE CONTEXT IN WHICH THE IMAGES ARE USED, DO NOT NECESSARILY REFLECT THE VIEWS OR POLICY OF, NOR IMPLY APPROVAL OR ENDORSEMENT BY, THE UNITED STATES HOLOCAUST MEMORIAL MUSEUM"

Library of Congress Cataloging in Publication Data

Gabor, Ebi, 1927-
    The blood tattoo.

    (Woman in history, ISSN 0195-8743 ; v. 85)
    Includes index.
    1. Gabor, Ebi, 1927 -   2. Holocaust, Jewish
(1939-1945)- Hungary - Personal narratives.
3. Jews-Hungary-Personal narratives.
Woman in history; 85.
D810-J4G24   1987   D40.53'15'039240439   87-24840
ISBN 0-930383-11-7 (pbk.)

Monument Press
4565 E. Mallory Ave, Memphis, TN, 38117
901.328.7206
www.monumentpress.net
publisher@monumentpress.net

In Memory of

My father, Mor Grünblatt   My brothers, Laci and Tibi

In Honor of

My mother, Margaret Grünblatt

and
for the Love of

My children, Ronald M. Monitz and Erika Baum

and

My loving husband, Jeno Gabor and brother Barna

With the sincere wish that
eventually my two children will
have the strength to read this book.

iv

Acknowledgements

To my son Ronny: *Words are not ample to express my gratitude, for without your suggestion for this book, and without your coaxing and persuading, this book would never have been written. For your enormous help along the way, for your continuous faith in me, for your encouragement, and for your legal services and advise, my deepest thanks—and to God for making you mine.*

To my dearest Mother: *Whose faith in God never faltered, for your guidance and unceasing encouragement when my faith was gone, for your constant consolation during our horrifying days and nights in the Nazi death camps whenever I was ready to give up, for your enormous love that kept me alive, I am endebted for the rest of my life. I love you.*

To my Husband, Jeno Gabor: *For your love and understanding during those difficult days and nights while reliving the horrifying experience, for the courage and faith you continuously had in me, for supporting me throughout the writing of this book; for your tremendous confidence in me and in this book, giving me the necessary strength to continue and finish it—all of my deepest gratitude.*

To Andy Baum, my Grandson: *For his steadfast confidence and cheers, for his giant generosity in offering to help me, a generation of maturity beyond his tender age of thirteen; for his steady encouragement and pride in me—a special thank you!*

To Captain Steven Green, my Nephew: *For his enthusiasm, his confidence and faith in me and in this book that he himself generated working towards the publication of this book, I am forever grateful.*

A special thanks to Dr. Arthur Frederick Ide: *Who oversaw the final editing and correction of the manuscript preparing it for publication; for his tireless efforts on behalf of this book, and the speedy conclusion of its publication, I am endebted.*

Table of Contents

Preface vii

Chapter One 1
Home—April 1944

Chapter Two 15
Kallosemeny—April 1944

Chapter Three 35
The Nyiregyhaza Ghetto—May 1944

Chapter Four 57
The Boxcar—May 1944

Chapter Five 71
Auschwitz—May 1944

Chapter Six 99
Boxcar to Plassow—June 1944

Chapter Seven 109
Plassow—June 1944

Chapter Eight 161
Back to Auschwitz—September 1944

Chapter Nine 169
Augsburg—September 1944

Chapter Ten 183
Muhldorf—March 1945

Chapter Eleven 197
Liberation. . . . . April 30, 1945

Epilogue 205

Index. 206

Author's Preface

I want to address a subject that has never been explored in detail. It is not easy. Although it has been 40 years, since I survived the Holocaust, I find it very painful to describe my day-to-day existence as a prisoner of the Nazi death camps. Yet it was the daily routine of terror, hunger, filth, and disease that made the Holocaust the living hell that it was.

The purpose of my story is not necessarily to bear witness. God knows that there are and have been many distinguished and eminent writers who have fulfilled this role. There are also numerous survivors who have been interviewed, Allied servicemen who have recounted their experiences in liberating the concentration camps, and prisoners like me on railroad tracks who have left memoirs for historians to chronicle the Holocaust, as I now do, and it is these works that keep alive the fragile flame of truth to hold before the world a light to keep it from ever forgetting the darkness that once settled across Europe and the Near East to cover one man's quest to erase an entire race.

What I do not find in the Holocaust literature is any account that explains to my satisfaction the feelings and the details of the degradation that millions lived through, and that millions more suffered for a time—then died from that experience. Until now it was simply unbearable to talk about it—especially in any detail. The effort to talk about it, and to write about it, requires the emotional strength to relive it. Some of us (we the survivors) will never muster such strength. For others, such as myself, time had to pass.

The memories and the imprint of the horror on the soul can never go away. It was not only horror but despair and degradation too profound for anyone who experienced it to forget, as I witness now in this book. But for those who did not see with their own eyes the monstrosities of the Holocaust, and did not experience the petrifying fear and agony of not only standing before Mengele during his "selection process," or feel the butt of wrath of enraged SS, this book, I hope, will bring it closer to them so that they too can understand the living hell millions of people knew before they suffered a cruel and merciless death by gas, bullet or various tortures.

This book is not a history book. This book is a human life

account, a true story of a mortal struggle to survive. It is a story of Birkenau, a part of the Auschwitz death camp that existed solely to destroy human dignity and life. It is a true tale of Auschwitz, Augsburg, and other camps like Birkenau where I cheated death numerous times.

With Auschwitz, Birkenau, and camps in between, came unwanted memories. The experiences I had in each hell hole have been engraved in my memory. Now I have found the courage and the strength to summon to consciousness these same memories to write this book, so that in my own way I may make it a little bit harder for the world to forget.

—Ebi Gabor

Los Angeles, California

Ebi
Three months after liberation.

Chapter One

Home — April 1944

The first knock came at 2 o'clock in the morning. It was followed, in rapid succession, by other knocks: fists banging against the front door and the bedroom windows. Why they didn't ring the bell we still don't know. I heard my father telling Mommy not to worry. Maybe it was another fire on the estate. Fires on the farm happened occasionally, and my father was the estate director. He would have to be told. But at 2 in the morning? Nothing ordinary was supposed to happen at 2 in the morning. Not even ordinary emergencies.

"Go back to bed. Go back to sleep," I heard my father say to Mom. "I will get dressed and go and see."

The knocking continued feverishly. I got out of bed and stood by the bedroom door, looking down the hall to the living room. My brother Barna was up, too, also watching. Barna was 17 years old. I was three years younger.

Dad, in his pants and pajama top, opened the door. Before him stood a very tall gendarme, looking even taller than his actual height by the effect of the distinctive cock tail feather protruding from his Hungarian policeman's hat. Expressionless eyes looked out from a long face.

On either side of the gendarme stood a similar figure: each shorter in height and their features not as clear to me as I stood watching, looking past my father from down the hall.

"Hi, Stefan," my father said, recognizing the tall one, greeting him warmly.

"What can I do for you at such an unusually early hour?"

The gendarmes stood motionless and silent for a moment.

"This is not an official visit," said the tall one.

"Oh, I realize that," responded father. "At 2 in the morning how could it be?"

Suddenly, all three officers, members of the special police

(called the gendarmes) came through the doorway, pushing my father aside.

They walked into the living room. My father followed. He looked pale and out of breath.

The last gendarme through the opened door looked familiar to me. At least his face did. Then it hit me. It was my best friend's father: Kato's father. My mother and father often socialized with him.

Now Mom was up. Entering the living room, she instantly recognized Kato's father. She went toward him to greet him with the customary embrace. Kato's father raised his palm. He shook his head no. Mom and Dad exchanged looks of bewilderment. Both were puzzled at this unusual occurance.

Father kept talking in the familiar fashion of a man among friends. It was as if the nasty moment at the front door hadn't happened.

"I am glad to see you, fellows. Glad you stopped by, despite the hour," father declared.

"Mother," father paused. "Get some cognac, please, for my friends here."

The tall gendarme held up a hand, but Dad kept talking.

"You see, I wanted to look you up in the morning, anyway. But this is better. I'd rather talk about it here. You saved me a trip to town."

"Stefan," my father spoke to the gendarme in charge, "they want to take away my Tibi. They want to take him away from me and I would like to ask your opinion. Could you help me? Could you do something for me, please?"

Tibi was 19. The age for young Jewish men to report to labor camps had been lowered a few days ago from 21 to 18. It had been one of the first orders announced by the Germans after the occupation of Hungary on March 19, 1944. But that was in Debrecen, 80 miles away, where Tibi and I had been staying with our aunt and our cousins. Maybe it was different here out in the country, thought my father, where he knew people and had influence.

3

"I need your help, Stefan. Of course, I don't want to do it for nothing. I'm ready to pay any price, any, any price, Stefan, just please help me." The gendarme looked at my father as if questioning his sanity. Still my father talked, taking the policeman's disapproving look as a warning that there were people around, his colleagues, and now was not the time to be offering a bribe.

"You know what I mean, Stefan. Your superiors," my father continued with a knowing look. "Those who can take care of it. You tell them, please. Tell them I'll pay any price. I'm willing and ready to pay. Stefan, will you please do that for me?"

The gendarmes watched my father as he tried to buy his son's safety, their faces morbid, motionless. Each of my first two brothers had seen this day coming. Laci had left Hungary in 1940 and tried to go to Palestine. He was caught in Bulgaria, returned to Hungary, and then left again—this time heading north, and had been gone ever since.

Even as a little girl I remembered the loud, frightening arguments just before Laci left home. "Father, don't you realize they're killing Jews in Poland already, and soon they will be doin it everywhere in Europe?" And, my father replying, "Not here. It will not happen here. Hungary is a civilized country."

And Tibi. Brave, handsome, my hero Tibi—whom I had seen with my own eyes fight back against the Jew-hating thugs, the Arrow-Cross, in the streets of Debrecen. "Pull his pants down, and let's see if he's a Jew," two of them taunted as a group of us walked home one day in 1943. Tibi was on them in a flash, smashing their heads with brass knuckles on both hands until we begged him to stop.

And now my proud, patriotic father, who had shouted at Laci that our leaders were not monsters, looked into the dull faces of the village gendarmes and seemed finally to begin to see there for the first time the truth of our fate.

For the events that followed, I had at the time no words to describe the shock, the petrifying panic, the horror from the helplessness, and the anguish from the vileness of life on the verge of death that was to consume our family, first my father and mother and very shortly all of us.

A look of terror was on my father's face now, his eyes literally bulging from their sockets. Mom saw Dad's eyes and broke into sobs. Barna and I stood off to the side and constantly searched each other's eyes for answers to the things we heard and saw but did not understand.

We watched and listened, afraid to go closer, at the same time unable to stay away. Hearing mother's cry we both ran to help her and hold her and try to console her. Dad noticed us and tried to shoo us back to our rooms.

But I had caught the eye of Kato's dad and rushed over to greet him. He was polite but not his usual warm self, not letting me get near enough to touch him. The gendarme in charge, the tall one, seemed to notice the close relationship. There was, or had been, a close relationship with all the village police when they paid official visits to the estate and received favors from my father—fresh food from the farm, a cool drink, hunting trips.

I asked Kato's father how Kato was doing. I had not seen her for six months. "Would you please tell Kato that I would like to see her soon?" I asked.

Kato's father gave no reply. I looked up at him startled and stung by his insult. The silence and emotions of the moment were something that the gendarme in charge did not want to cope with. He stiffened. The stern look in his face became even more stern.

"Let's get on with it so we can get it over with faster," he barked. "We have been sent here with the official duty to take inventory of your personal property...."

Before he could go on, my father sprang to his feet and stood directly in front of the gendarme. Placing the palms of his hands on his chest, my father cried out over and over, "My personal property? The fruits of my labor? You want to take inventory of that?"

The policeman nodded affirmatively. The other two stepped back and averted their eyes. Mom moved closer to Dad, trying to grasp his arm and calm him. Father's questions continued and now he was hitting his chest with his palms for emphasis.

"Whatever I have I worked very hard for, and you come here to take inventory?"

"Morris, I am only following orders." He spoke softly and politely.

"Orders? Whose orders?"

"The department."

"The department? Now? In the middle of the night?" Again the one in charge nodded yes.

"But why should anybody want to know about my personal wealth? Whose damn business is that? Would I ask you about yours?"

The policeman stared for a moment with a look of wonder, then turned to the two others and asked, "Am I dreaming? Is this real? Doesn't this man realize what's happening to him?" The amazement in his eyes was genuine, and seemed only natural, because to me, too, the pleading of my father seemed like something out of a frightening dream.

"You can't come in here awakening me and my family in the middle of the night.... You tell me I must understand. I'm afraid I don't understand."

The tall policeman grasped my father by the shoulders. "Morris," he said, trying to be soothing. "Morris, we must get on with it. My colleagues and I have a rough day ahead of us."

"What in the world is it that you want to see?"

"It's not me who wants to see, Morris. It is the Hungarian government that wants to know."

"But couldn't it have waited until morning?" my father asked. All three shrugged.

The wide look of terror in my father's face keeps alive the memory of that night, one of the most fearful of all my recollections that came before and after. Before I decided to write about the terrible years of 1944 nd 1945 in my life, many times I tried to put out of my mind that first night of humiliation and fear. It was a memory I could never shake and is the reason why each occurance and word of conversation comes back vividly as I write.

The officer in charge motioned my father to sit next to him and the other two at the dining table.

"I must ask you Morris, in order not to prolong the agony for both of us, to bring out all your cash, jewelry and other valuables and put them on the table. Don't worry. I will give you a receipt for every item."

Silently now, my father complied, bringing from other rooms the cash he had in the house. One of the officers counted and the other wrote on a piece of paper.

Stefan asked, "Morris, is there some money you forgot about, perhaps?"

"Not that I know of."

"What about your wallet?"

"You're saying to me that you intend to take every last *filler* of mine?"

"Those are my orders." My father emptied his wallet of the few notes it contained.

The two other policemen muttered some words we could not hear then one of them got up from the table and walked to the wall, lifted off a picture: a painting of a rural scene. He carried it back to the table and handed it to his friend. "Here it is," he said.

"What are you doing with the picture?" my mother asked.

"Oh, he likes it. He likes it very much," said the policeman who had gone to the wall.

"Yes. I like it very much."

"What are you doing with it?" my mother questioned.

"Nothing. He gave it to me," said the policeman pointing to his friend.

"But it was not his to give," my mother protested.

"Oh yes it was, and now it's mine," said the gendarme, talking like a stranger. He was Kato's father.

My mother, nervous and worried looking, went to my father who, by now, was at the wall safe on the other side of the room with the gendarme in charge beside him. Dad had not seen the policeman take the picture.

My father turned to my mother, but Stefan grabbed Dad's arm and ordered him to keep working on the safe to get it opened. My father, in anger, shoved the hand away and moved to my mother's side. She was crying again.

"What happened?" my father demanded of the other two policemen.

"Nothing happened. She's just frightened," one of the policemen responded. "Let's get on with it. Let's get this mess over with."

"Right. Enough delays," barked another.

The tone of all three was now threatening. Dad looked at us giving the signal with his eyes not to object or protest or try to stop them. He was afraid they would strike one of us if we delayed them any longer.

When Dad finally put the family jewelry on the table, all pretense of carrying out a reluctant duty vanished. The policemen attacked like sharks.

"I want this one."

"This is mine!"

They were now placing rings on their fingers: three or four at a time, modeling them, seeing which ones looked best, which to choose from.

"Weren't you supposed to be taking inventory only?" my father asked. "You seem to be taking it for yourselves. How can I be accounted for that? How can I ever get these things back?"

They all looked up from the table at my father like he was a crazy man who still didn't understand what was happening to him. Stefan tried again for calm. "Don't worry about it. Just don't worry about it."

The formalities of official, rational procedures were abandoned completely now. The policemen were not only robbing my father of the family's possessions and of his dignity, but were rendering him insane as well for insisting on receipts and the procedures of a mere inventory. Couldn't he see? they seemed to be saying: He is doomed and should have realized it from the beginning.

By now, at 3:30 in the morning, my father did realize that his reasoning was to no avail, that reason was being turned to impossible ravings of a madman. The fear of the unknown was upon him now, more so than the sense of loss of mere possessions. But his composure was back somewhat, enough so that his deepest fears could not be seen in his proud face just then. He was concentrating on consoling my mother.

Barna and I stood there helpless and bewildered, watching our mother walking like a zombie from room to room, Dad trying to soothe her, but she was not hearing.

At 4 a.m., the chief of police, my father's hunting partner and friend, arrived at our door. Oh, Dad was so happy to see him. Naively, he believed that the chief would call a halt to the outrages, stop all that had happened and prevent all the bad that might happen in time to come. My father was like a child looking for the kiss that would make the hurt go away.

The chief was full of apologies and assurances that the inconvenience would soon be over.

My father stood before his friend and covered his eyes with the palms of his hands.

"Can I go back to sleep, Robbie, and will you tell me when it's over?"

"No," said the chief, "but there is nothing really to worry about."

"Why are you taking away the things then? Everything I worked for all my life," father asked, again his voice full of despair.

"Oh, we will give you a receipt for everything, Morris, and when the war is over you will get back every item. I'll personally make sure of that."

His next words did not inspire confidence.

"Oh, by the way, fellows, did you remember to put the gun collection in the inventory?" At which the chief led the way to the gun case in the next room, opened the glass door and removed my father's hunting guns one by one. "Oh, I love this one. Hey, Morris, I never saw this before. Is it a new one?"

The chief, caressing each one lovingly, commented on all the several rifles and shotguns in the case, then turned to his three subordinates. "Would you like to have this? This is a dandy gun: I used it often," and, without asking my father or looking at him, the chief handed each one a gun from the collection.

"Don't worry, Morris," he said when the cabinet was empty, "When you return, I promise you I will bring back every one. And now, Morris, I must ask you and the family to come with us."

"Come with you, Robbie? Come with you where?"

"We have orders to take you and your family to the Jewish temple until we collect everybody from all the neighboring towns."

"Temple? Family? Robbie, what is this?"

"It's nothing, just here into town to the Jewish synagogue."

"I don't feel like praying," my father said tartly.

"Oh, I know, not for that reason, but I've got orders. Take everybody to the temple."

"And for how long?" my father asked. "And when? And why?"

"Well, you're asking me things I don't know myself. I can only surmise that probably they want to gather all the Jews together to find out how many live in this area."

"That's all?" my father asked.

"I guess so. What other reasons would there be? Anyway, Morris, it hurts me more than words can say, but I have no choice but to tell you now that in the name of the Hungarian government, you and your family are under arrest and you must accompany us at once."

"What are the charges? What did I do?"

"I don't know. I know only that my orders are to arrest all Jews and take them to the town's Jewish temple. You must be there at 6 a.m."

"What is the rush?" my father wanted to know. "Why no warning, no time to prepare?"

"Because," responded the chief, "they wanted to make sure that we got Morris Grünblatt and his family first."

"Why me first?"

"Because the higher-ups believe that you are a well-known and respected person around here and you have a lot of Christian friends like me, and you may use your connections to get away if given time."

"I, a patriotic Hungarian, the most decorated soldier of the First World War, loyal to this country like no other man? I would run away? Where to, Robert? Where would I go? This is my home. Robert, please assure your superiors for me that I have no intention to run away."

Father continued. "I never believed the day would come when I would need to protect myself and my fellow man or my country. I'll do anything that is asked of me peacefully, but please don't hurt my family."

"Don't worry. I will personally see to that. And your house keys will always be with me," the chief interjected, dangling the keys on his finger.

Deceit after deceit. From taking inventories to simply taking. From "Oh, it's nothing to worry about," to, "You are under arrest." What next from this long and trusted friend?

"Tell me, my friend," Dad asked in hope, "I may still call you that—my friend?"

"Of course, Morris," the chief affirmed, putting a hand on my father's shoulder. "Absolutely, I'll always be your friend. Don't you worry, Morris." The three gendarmes were openly ransacking our home as the chief gave his assurances. Kato's father chuckled and said what a mess it all was, and I wondered, What kind of person is this? What is he made of? I had sat at his table in his home and he had made me welcome. The chief ordered us to take one set of extra clothing and some food, and he suggested that we each take a coat. As the gendarmes kicked the furniture around and tossed our belongings into piles, with the chief standing there beside us and our small bundles and a bit of food in a paper bag, my father gave a terrifying appearance. A man of only 49, independent of mind, a figure of authority who towered in my estimation, he stood now degraded and humiliated—about to be driven from his home. Even animals are allowed their shelters. Barna and I realized his pain and he saw this in us, for he reached and hugged us both, one in each arm, and the hug was so tight that it almost hurt.

"These are my most precious things. Don't ever try to take them away."

"Nobody will, Morris. I assure you."

Barna, frightened, terrified like the rest of us, tried to hide his tears and console mother.

"Tell me, Robert," my father asked, his voice getting louder, "Which God shall I ask for help—yours or mine? I think yours, for mine has forsaken me."

Everyone stopped and stared at my father. Barna and I wondered if he was gone mad. Father saw the silent panic he had caused, and said quickly, feigning humor, "Oh, yeah. That's right. I forgot. We have no choice. You're taking us to the Jewish temple. Should I consider that Heaven or Hell?"

"A mixture of both, maybe," entoned my father and Barna simultaneously.

"You won't be staying there long," offered the chief.

"And you tell me not to be concerned...." father mocked.

"Please, for God's sake!" my mother cried. The house became deadly silent for a moment.

"My friend," father spoke softly, as much to himself as to the chief, "When human dignity is ignored, as you know and I know, the result is human catastrophe."

"You can count on me."

"Can I? Okay, then stop them." My father pointed at the gendarmes. "Tell them to go away."

"That, unfortunately, I cannot do. That is beyond my jurisdiction or control."

My father slumped, exhausted, no more hopeless entreaties left in him. The pitiful sight of him must have moved some part of the soul of his so-called friend, because the chief ordered the gendarmes dismissed.

They looked confused. "It's all right," the chief announced. "I will take personal responsibility."

As the door closed behind them, my father's brain released the last of his defenses. He buried his face in his hands and stood leaning against a door frame. His body shook and he sobbed uncontrolably. To this day, and despite all that followed, my father crying in fear and helplessness is the most heartbreaking sight I ever saw. I never imagined such a thing could happen. We joined him with our own flow of tears in those last minutes at home, not caring that the chief was standing there watching.

The chief honestly tried to console my father, but he seemed to realize that his presence was a further humiliation and he stepped away, allowing time for Dad to compose himself.

It was time to go now. We walked through our dismantled home room by room for a final goodbye.

As we reached to pick up our packages, the chief stopped us. "Leave everything. I'll send somebody for it and have it delivered to you at the temple this afternoon. I want you to walk like a man, the man that you are."

"Thank you," my father said in barely a whisper.

Before we reached the door, the chief stopped us again. "Morris, do you have any money?"

"I have 10 *pengo*. That's all what they left me. Would you like to have that, too? They took all my money from Margit's purse, also" father concluded, referring to my mother.

"I don't want anything from you, Morris. I want to give you

whatever I have with me," and he handed my father about 50 *pengo*, the equivalent of about ten dollars. "You won't need this right now, but just in case, you should have it. I will put more in your clothes pockets before I send them to you. I will send more packages to you later the same way. Watch the pockets of anything I send, all right?"

Again my father thanked him.

"What is to become of my farm stock? Who will see that they are fed and cared for?"

"Don't worry. They will all be taken care of, even if I have to send out my own men to do it."

We were out of the door now. The chief was turning the key in the lock.

My father looked at him. "Tell me the truth. Are you taking me to my ignoble end?"

"Morris, please forgive me. It is my job, my duty. Do you think I enjoy this? Why did they choose me to come and get you? Do you know?"

"I don't. But you do."

"No, I don't. Believe me, they are punishing me as well."

And with these heartfelt words, my father's best friend led him to the gateway of our hell.

I was 14 years old, almost 15, on that early morning in April of 1944 when the village police chief led us away from our home. None of us knew why or for how long we would be gone. None of us even in the darkest moments of those first hours after the police came imagined that we would never see this home again. Least of all me, the baby of the family, naive and with a head filled more with my first puppy love than the fact that Germany had invaded my country. When the Germans ordered all Jews to stitch a yellow Star of David to our clothes, I stitched the first one to a summer dress and joked with my cousin Magda in Debrecen, "Now we will be able to see which good-looking guy is a Jew."

So we turned away from the huge and beautiful estate, the second that my father had managed in recent years, where he was the director and supervised the tending of dozens of crops. Wheat, corn, sugar beets, fruits and tobacco grew there on thousands and thousands of acres. And the most enchanting sight of all was a castle across a field from us, built hundreds of years ago. Like our house, the castle was built on a slight knoll on the flat farming land of this part of Hungary. The titled family that owned the castle no longer lived there, my father told me. We turned away from the door not for a moment suspecting that we were leaving forever also.

Hitler's victory in Czechoslovakia was only a prelude to the fear and aggression which many nations experienced under the force of Axis conquest.

Chapter Two

Kallosemeny – April 1944

In the early hours of the morning, we rode in the police chief's horse-drawn carriage the two or three miles to the town of Kallosemeny and were deposited outside the gate of the Jewish temple. A few Arrow-Cross men with rifles on their shoulders were walking around the temple yard. The police chief introduced my father to them. They greeted us with a polite hello.

Walking toward the temple's main entrance I saw that the benches from inside had been removed and were stacked against the outside of the building, leaving the floor inside clear to make way for the Jews who would be rounded up from neighboring towns. On the floor was ordinary straw, the same as I had seen under the horses and cows at home. It did not register with me at first that now we, too, were expected to sleep on straw.

I had never been in this temple before. Father was engaged in a friendly conversation with one of the Arrow-Cross men. There was no panic at the moment, so Barna and I and Mom took a look around and saw religious objects up close for the first time (like the Torah and the Ark). We remarked how delicate the objects were. I had been to temples before, in Debrecen. Going to the temple, for me, was mostly an occasion to meet friends and watch boys and have the boys look at me. Mostly, we had sat on the steps while the grownups were inside. The few times we had gone in were only to ask for money to buy a drink or a snack.

In a couple of hours the news was out that the Jews were being brought to the temple. Slowly the townspeople began to congregate around the temple to watch the Jews being rounded up and herded into the temple confines. My father called those who watched "the silent majority."

By early afternoon the town's Jews began to arrive. Dad and

Barna knew all of them. I knew only the boys and girls close to my age. We greeted each other happily, "Here we are again," for we had spent the day together just the day before, and in fact had caused a delay in the Passover observance because we were off horseback riding. Mother had been furious and harassed me before, during, and after the Passover supper—for us the last supper at home.

Old men and women and younger women and their children were brought to the temple gate and directed inside by the arresting police officers. The young ones were being very noisy, frightened by the new surroundings and new faces, constantly running and burying their heads, crying, in their mothers' laps. The children who were a little older, the ones about 6 to 10 years old, were running all over the temple yard, and managed to tip over one of the piles of benches. The heavy boards landed on some of the children, who cried and shrieked, causing a commotion right from the beginning.

With people being brought in and accidents like this happening, some of the parents wanted to know why didn't the Arrow-Cross bring in the local doctor with the first arrivals instead of the local grocer. An Arrow-Cross with a gun on his shoulder marched up and down like a guard at Buckingham Palace. He paused and then shrugged his shoulders. He didn't know. And he didn't care.

The rabbi showed up in mid-afternoon. Upon seeing people everywhere, sitting on tipped-over piles of benches, wandering in and out of the temple, he raised his palms to the sky and began praying out loud in Hebrew and crying bitterly. It was an outrage against the house of God. It must stop immediately.

Some elders joined him. Others just watched. The children ignored him. The guards, who were drawn from the locality, knew the rabbi. They ignored his outburst. They did not interfere. But my father did, interrupting to the point that he shouted that hysterical behavior could be dangerous, that God isn't deaf—God, father affirmed, can hear silent prayers just as easily as loud ones.

That comment was a mistake on my father's part. The small and elderly rabbi looked up at my dad and at the top of his lungs he shouted, "How would you know, you goy! When have you ever set foot in a temple? What do you know about God?"

"My knowledge has nothing to do with what I am asking you," answered father very quietly, but in perfect Yiddish, trying to show the respect due the rabbi.

It was too big a surprise for the old man, I guess, to hear this man who never came to the temple, standing there in his distinctly non-Jewish attire—riding britches and boots—speaking in the Jewish tongue. He looked as if he was going to collapse.

Dad reached for the rabbi's arm to keep him from falling. "Are you okay?" he kept asking the rabbi. The commotion had attracted a crowd. The rabbi was regaining his composure—enough so that he wanted to check if he had heard correctly. He asked questions in Yiddish. Dad answered. They conversed easily. It was as much a shock to me as it was to the rabbi.

I knew my father could pray in Hebrew. I also knew he did not understand Hebrew. What none of us knew was that he mastered Yiddish.

My father never denied his Jewish beliefs. He had told us many times that the Ten Commandments were his law and our law. But "religion," he told us, was "a private thing, between a man and his conscience." "For God, anything," he would say. "For religion, nothing."

My father tried now to reason with the religious people in the temple courtyard that any deviation from normal behavior would risk reinforcements of Arrow-Cross guards, different ones —and this would mean disaster. With so many little children already creating chaos and confusion the guards could become violent. "So, for everybody and for the children's sake, let's not rock the boat," Dad instructed, and for awhile everyone stayed calm.

By 5:30 that evening the temple's courtyard was full of people, strangers to one another mostly, except that all were

Jews arrested and forced to come here like us. Some prayed. Some took one look into the temple and turned and hurried out because the interior meant different things to different people. What we all had in common in equal measure was the fear of the unknown.

As the hours passed, little cliques started to form. But all had the same question. "How do they expect us to sleep? And where?" Someone pointed inside.

"On the straw there? Next to each other?"

"You must be kidding," I heard one woman exclaim. "I don't even know these people."

"Wait, let me introduce you," someone said, sarcastically.

For us teenagers there was another question. None of us dared to ask, but all were curious to know: How could so many strangers sleep in such a small area? Who would be close to whom? Someone suggested maybe we would all be sent home to sleep, and everybody broke up in loud laughter.

The teenagers socialized. The little ones were frightened. Babies cried. The old ones prayed. The grownups, like my parents, sat around wherever they could find space and wondered and speculated. Why were we here? When would it end so we could return to our homes?

Everybody had their suitcases and hand baggage next to them, a pitiful sight, painful to recall. Suitcases too big for their meager contents, disfigured, discolored from wear and tear. Most were wrapped around several times with twine to hold them together. Bits of fabric stitched hurriedly together held the immediate needs of many.

Some children's toys became scattered over the ground and soon all the children tried to claim them as their own. By early afternoon the parents got into a fight protecting their children's possessions.

Mom pleaded with Dad not to get involved when he tried to reason with them. "I must try to protect them as well as ourselves," he explained.

Physical fights between parents were dangerous, my dad

reasoned. Among the curiosity seekers surrounding the temple were some plain thugs. Anything could set them off. Violence among the Jews could surely provoke them. Dad wanted the fights—if there had to be fights—kept well inside, out of sight to the people watching outside.

"Please listen to me, and listen good," Dad warned everyone. He knew he had gained credibility as someone special when the chief of police and his family came to the temple earlier carrying in suitcase after suitcase for us. He was hoping his words would be heeded.

"If you are going to be loud and behave ridiculously, it will give them an excuse to attack us. These hoodlums guarding us only know how to hold guns. But the gendarmes know also how to use them. Why do we play with our fate? It will come soon enough anyway."

For a while everyone seemed to listen to Dad. The noisy ones quieted down. It was not destined to last, however. When night came, the fighting would resume over space on the temple floor.

The number of onlookers outside grew by sundown to several hundred, some of them looking for "our Jews," as the expression went, to give them, along with a kind word, bundles of bread, hard-boiled eggs and raw vegetables. Everyone inside said the same thing about the food: Never mind, we brought plenty from home. If only they and we had known how welcome the extra food would have been in the days ahead.

The nervousness, the anxiety, were apparent in all now toward evening. Everybody's mouth was busy constantly, either eating or talking. The noise was deafening.

Dad placed our suitcases in a temple storage room arranged through the police chief. Welcome to the advantage of being the first ones hauled in, my father weakly joked. When nightfall came Dad and Barna brought four benches for us to sleep on in the storage room.

Outside, in the temple proper, there was confusion that turned to chaos. The idea of spending the night away from home had not sunken in very well. Everyone had stayed away from the inside of the temple after taking a first look in there during the day. Their belongings were in the courtyard right next to them so there had been no reason for them to go in. Somehow, I guess, nobody thought of the coming night except the teenagers, who all went in at once and secured for their parents and themselves the most desireable spots, next to each other and against the walls, leaving only the center part of the room available to everyone else.

The older ones at once delared that they were entitled to a wall space. The parents of babies and little children claimed they should have a wall space, so nursing mothers would not be on public display. The elders agreed with that, but the walls weren't theirs to offer in the first place, so nobody moved. The rabbi tried to appease everybody, but it seemed to me no one was listening to him, either.

As the hundreds crowded into the temple tried to settle down for the night, there would be a moment of silence, and then someone would move, making a strange sound on the straw. We stood at the doorway watching. Little children in the middle of the floor cried to go to the bathroom. Their parents would scoop them up in their arms and try to get across the floor to the door, stepping on someone else's child on the way.

"Fancy people like you should stay at the Ritz—where you don't have to watch where you're going."

"You imbecile!" would come the retort.

"Rabbi, do something! There is no justice," added a voice of someone else rudely awakened.

"Mr. Rosenblum, you are looking for perfect justice?"

"Can you tell me a better place I should look, Rabbi?"

"Cut it out!" another cut in. "We are trying to forget and go to sleep."

Yet another voice cried out, "You think you can dream it away? Try it! Maybe when you wake up in the morning it won't be there."

The sun was breaking the horizon when we awoke and

heard noises. Dad wanted to investigate but Mom stopped him. She felt safe in the privacy of the little storage space in the jumble of cardboard boxes, brooms, garbage pails, pieces of broken lamps, a broken desk, and other junk. It was heaven compared to the straw and the wall to wall people of the big room. But we couldn't open the windows, so we only stayed there to sleep or eat.

The police chief had packed two cushions and two blankets in a suitcase for us, explaining that we should share the bedding and keep another suitcase only for food, which he packed with jars of different things to eat. Another suitcase was for Barna and Dad's things. The fourth was for Mom and me. The chief said that he did not bring any more packages because he was unsure of future transportation and if he had to walk any distance it would be difficult.

"Don't use the food yet. Save it until I know where they are taking you, and whether I will be able to take food to you. As long as you are here, I will bring food every day."

My father promised to repay the chief when all this was over.

"Let's not worry about that," the chief responded.

His wife and son came three times a day with food and words of encouragement. At night he came, like so many others because now we were his Jews.

We remained at the temple three days and two nights while every Jew for 35 miles around was brought in. We were about 250 people in all by now, when two gendarmes we did not know and a few from the local Arrow-Cross entered the temple ground and ordered us to line up, in rows four or five people wide. Everyone, naturally, loaded up with as much as he or she could carry, or as much as the gendarmes would allow.

"Where are we going?" everyone wanted to know.

"For a walk." spat a gendarme sarcastically.

The gendarmes and the Arrow-Cross started pushing and shoving us. Some of the Jews at first wouldn't move, wanting to stay in the sanctuary of the temple grounds.

"On your feet. Up, up, everybody up!" the gendarmes shouted. They shoved their riffle muzzles hard into the people sitting on their suitcases, and with each thrust, the people cried out, both in pain and humiliation.

On a cloudy morning in mid-April, the march began, and before long rain began to fall. Was it them or us God wanted to punish, or was it God's tears? The old people trudged along in heavy winter coats, not because it was cold but because with their other belongings in hand, there was no where else to carry them. Two women who had come to the temple on the last day wore expensive fur coats for the same reason. We wondered how it was possible that the coats had not been confiscated.

Parents with little children running beside them, running to stay with the march, pleased the gendarmes. "Slow down, please," parents pleaded, "just a little bit, for the children's sake."

"We haven't got all day," a gendarme snapped back, keeping the line moving swiftly.

The rain came harder and harder, forming puddles in the mud along the roadside. Kids ran to the puddles to play. Mothers with packages in hand ran after them, shrieking at the kids to get out of the mud. Gendarmes shouted at the mothers to get back in line.

We had thought of a lot of things to bring, but an umbrella wasn't one of them. No one had protection from the rain, pouring down now in sheets. Bundles bound in paper fell apart, the contents spilling into the road only to be trampled on.

"Oh, my God, oh, my God, help me!" wailed one woman as her possessions fell from her bundle.

A voice cried out from the back, "Leave God alone. Can't you see? God is in trouble. You are watching him die."

Involuntarily we all stopped at the shock the words caused. The gendarmes also stopped. They looked at each other, at a loss for words or orders, it seemed.

As the rabbi and the elders prayed, the gendarmes walked back along the ranks of marchers. "Who said that?" they demanded to know.

"Me, sir. It was me who said that," came a voice a couple of lines back from us. It had come from a man on crutches.

The gendarmes looked at him, maybe with pity, anyway with an emotion that surprised us. "You know something," one of them said, "I... I... I begin to think you are right."

Another took a loudspeaker to the front of the lines and announced that now was as good a time as any to stop and eat our lunch. Resting on our wet and muddy baggage we stopped at the edge of a village.

A first little children, then adults from the village ran to the roadside to stare. Just stare. No one asked who we were. No one protested. No one spoke. Just ... bystanders.

It was our first encounter with another town and its people, people who never read newspapers–not even if they could. The yellow stars we wore on our clothes meant nothing to them. I don't think our audience even knew what the stars were.

After about an hour the gendarmes ordered us back onto our feet. Mom had dug out some dry clothes for us. We changed and resumed our long damp journey.

The next half hour wasn't so bad. The younger ones helped the older ones with the packages which were getting heavier from the incessant rain. Still everyone kept going.

The real problem now was the grownups needing to relieve themselves. The lowland plains of Hungary are almost perfectly flat and empty. You can look in any direction for miles and hardly see a tree. Not much hope of privacy.

The men in the group were the religious elders and only a few were near Dad's age (in their forties), and these, except my father, were sick or handicapped. Otherwise they would have been in the labor camps like most Jewish men of 18, 17, and even 16 years old to 55 years old. That was why in our group my father was the only man suitable to assume any kind of leadership. Because of this my father was asked to approach the gendarmes to ask about some solution to the problem of the toilet, a problem which was becoming more severe by the minute. The gendarme in charge seemed to agree that something had to be done. "What do you suggest?" he asked my father. "Well, the trees don't offer privacy," father observed. "Only for the children. But one of these little villages should be able to help, don't you think?"

The gendarme appeared undecided. My father seized the opportunity. "We would be happy to pay for your kindness. Everyone, I am sure, would be glad to show their appreciation."

"Okay," said the gendarme, his assertiveness returning. "Why don't you handle it?" Dad placed some money in his hand immediately. "Go tell your people that you will be helping them with this. We'll stop at the next village."

By early afternoon the children were starting to tire from the walking and became cranky. Parents weighted down with baggage couldn't carry them. Other's couldn't help. They had their own problems.

Common courtesies had begun to diminish early in the march, and now insults and impatience with children's behavior (that was only to be expected) dominated the talk and the mood of everyone. Nerves were on edge and fatigue had overcome all but the strongest when at around dinnertime we arrived at a place in the prairie where huge barns were situated at odd angles to one another. We stopped. The only thing we felt at the moment was relief from the agony of the march.

We were ordered into one of the giant wooden barns, barns that I recognized as being used for the final stages of drying tobacco leaves. The ground looked familiar, too: more straw for us to sleep on. This time it was a welcomed sight. Parents scrambled madly to find the best resting spot, falling over their suitcases and toppling over each other with children under foot. The old ones cursed in the worst language of the gutter, ignoring the presence of the children.   Dad managed to get Mother, Barna and me to a far corner of the barn, which he found while everyone else fought for a space nearer the entrance.

We had no idea where we were. Mother prepared food, as did everyone else in our pitiful group. Food seemed our only comfort, now. And the supply was dwindling.

Again the question: When is this horror to end? Why does not someone stop it?

The scene around us was like the temple situation all over again—only worse. Dirty children clung to their just-as-filthy mothers whose maternal training to quiet a crying child had deserted them as the wailing echoed off the bleached wooden walls of the windowless barn.

Barna and I went out to look some more at this place of gloom. Dad followed soon after. More Jews were streaming into the other barns. Old men, women, children came in groups like ours. Some were walking in chains. Children lead blind relatives. Mothers walked with infants in arms. They dragged at their feet the same tattered suitcases and dingy bundles as the people in our group did. Teenagers arrived with rucksacks on their backs.

People came from all directions. As the numbers swelled, panic and chaos got worse. Children's screams were piercing and constant, not just in our barn but all through all the other barns. Hundreds of tiny ones screamed in fear and weariness in the strange surroundings. Some wandered and became separated from their mothers. Then the mothers would scream.

The whole place became like one terrified mouth howling in unheeded complaint across the flat bottomland of Hungary. To add insult to fright, other voices called out threateningly to "beat your brains out if you don't keep those brats quiet."

Barna and I looked up at Dad, looking for answers to explain the nightmare that we were living through and the nightmare of the hundreds and now thousands like us. Instead of answers, I saw in his face only sorrow and worry and I thought with what disgust he must be thinking of his fellow man at this moment as he watched the few men with guns on their shoulders patrolling the grounds, holding in their hands the fate of so many.

Around the collection yard with the barns was a barbed wire fence inside which we were allowed to wander. People strolled out of all the barns after they became settled and congregated to watch the new arrivals for friends and relatives.

We were several thousand already collected when, in the last batch to arrive, we saw my widowed grandmother and my aunt (whose husband was in a forced labor camp) from Debrecen. With them was also my other aunt who lived with Grandma. They had been together for the Passover holiday when they were picked up and brought eventually to this same collection point.

We ran to get Mom. When she heard the news of the arrival of Grandma and the aunts she was ecstatic. She saw her mother and smiled the first genuine smile since she had left home. After the hugs and kisses, the two mothers (mine and her's), spoke the same words at the same time: "Wait a minute. Here, my darling, I have brought you some food."

Everyone was so wrapped up in seeing one another we did not see the two men walk up to us until they were beside us. One was a German soldier. He was short, stout, with large, widely spaced blue eyes, sandy hair and short whiskers. The other was tall, skinny, dark-haired. He was an Hungarian Arrow-Cross soldier. Meeting the blond hair, blue eyed man was our first experience with a German. German soldiers had first appeared among us on our third day in the camp. Only a few Hungarian Jews knew the German language, so the Germans' orders came down through the local Arrow-Cross guards. From a distance the Germans seemed to behave in a more civilized manner than the Arrow-Cross thugs dressed up like soliders. Naturally, it was another deception at which the Germans were masters, for a more barbaric people than the German people I don't think ever existed in the history of the world.

Standing before us now, in his foreign-looking uniform with the letters SS on the jacket collar, the German soldier shouted something that none of us understood. He paused for a second, then gave my grandmother a rough shove and pointed, telling her apparently, to leave this part of the collection camp and go back to the group with which she had arrived. Grandma turned and faced these two imitations of human beings, and stared steadfastly into their hateful eyes.

With a gesture of off-hand disgust that an old woman would stand up to him, the German shoved my grandmother again—this time violently, knocking her sprawling on the ground. I had never seen such a barbaric, subhuman act in all my life, and the fat little toad of a German just stood their indifferently as if nothing had happened!

Mother and I rushed to help Grandma get up. "How can he be so evil?" Grandmother cried bitterly in Hungarian.

There was no answer. There was only a merry look of triumph from those terrorists looking down at the three of us.

This was the last time that I got close to Grandma in the ten days that we were in this collection camp. Once the Germans and the Arrow-Cross filled the barns, the people were sectioned off according to the districts that they had been brought from. Barbed wire separated the sections. When we saw Grandmother and my aunts after that we had to talk to them through the wire.

The scene during the day in the camp was something that had to be seen to be comprehended. Restless, noisy, haggard-looking people everywhere—short people, tall people, some fat and some slim, some light complexioned, refined and regal-looking, others dark-featured and showing the signs of a hard life. Every social and educational class was represented: intellectuals, merchants, farmers, workers, some who had been wealthy and some who had never been well off or comfortable.

In the midst of this gloom that hung over us there would be an occasional jolly smile, a joke, laughter to lighten for a moment the atmosphere of outrage mixed with gloom that was everywhere in the campground.

Bitter divisions erupted among us, too. Those involved in the most irreconcilable and the most troublesome disputes were people from different religious backgrounds. How ironic it was that we were humiliated, dehumanized, beaten and kicked because of the religion we had in common, yet one victim was ostracized by another for a different interpretation or practice of the same religion. Religious people, those who practiced their faith openly, sought out other religious people to make known their disapproval of those whose outward signs of religion they deemed to be insufficient. Others thought little of religion. They saw it as neither being good, nor being bad. They dwelled in self-pity, their thoughts turned to what now looked like a perilous fate. Their sole concern was how they could avoid it and survive. Then there were a very few, the extremely wealthy, who felt themselves doubly cheated by their fate. First, the wealth that they had so conveniently inherited from generation to generation was now gone. And, second, they had to suffer the humiliation of being thrown in with this common crowd.

During the first days of my imprisonment I watched as many people around me as I could, studying them wonderingly. I became absorbed in my watching, not only because I'd never seen so many different people in the same place, but because I was witnessing all the different signs of fear of which a human being is capable. People's eyes darted in every direction on the outlook for danger, whether there was reason or not. Then, when danger did come near, many would pretend not to recognize it. When pushed against one another by the guards, men and women politely straightened their clothes and hurried on.

Fear showed itself in restless, swift movements, constant nervous babble, and exaggerated gestures. Some gazed absently, some cursed sarcastically, when someone else in this sea of humanity washed into a small patch of space they had claimed as their own. Still others paid no attention to their surroundings, busying themselves instead with some imagined private matter that in their mind shut out the camp and its crowds. Some, whose eyes were red from crying, simply stood or sat trying to grab with trembling fingers every object that came within human reach. And everywhere children cried in their weary mother's arms.

It was at this time that I saw with my own eyes acts of

unspeakable horror that was beyond the capability of my young mind to accept as actually happening. Arrow-Cross hoodlums committed mutiliations and murders without provocation. They did it "just for the fun of it." They would simply wander among their terrified captives and stop and beat one of them to death with their gun butts. Their victims were usually the bearded, easily recognized religious Jews. Fingers were cut from hands. Whole arms were severed from living bodies. I saw one guard run his bayonet into the eye of a woman.

We wanted to believe that these atrocities were isolated. that they were the cruelties of deranged individuals acting behind the backs of their superiors. And it was true that the Germans did not approve—they wanted enough fear in us so that we would obey them without panicking. They wanted our trip to our final destination to take place efficiently. But these things we figured out later. We still had no clue of what history was yet to make of our destiny.

During the day on the outside of the wire fence the buzz of curiosity seekers could be heard from early morning on. There were still a few who continued to bring food for "their Jews." Some of the Jews who received food from outside the camp sold it to others. This sale of the food was a thriving business that capitalized on the misery of others.

The Germans supplied us with no food at all. When the Hungarian gendarmes went into the homes to take away the people they suggested that their victims take along a "few days" supply of food, but for many the "few days" were gone and so was their stock of hard-boiled eggs, bread and marmalade. Parents panicked when their supplies got down to the last scraps. Frantically pulling the arms of the gendarmes they asked how they were expected to feed their children. The gendarmes shrugged and pushed the pleading mothers' hands away.

A week had passed by now and the hunger and the fear of hunger swept the camp with the vengeance of a tornado. In our camp it was decided to pool the stocks of remaining food and to feed the children first. It was the only decent act that happened in that God-forsaken place.

The tired mothers, screaming for food for their hungry children were the wives of men who had been shipped out to the slave labor camps—most of the recent captives having been sent to the Russian front. Most of these men were fathers who would spend the war years not knowing that their wives and babies had been murdered in the gas chambers of Auschwitz on May 22, 1944.

But for now the questions for which there were no answers concerned the agonies of the living. Why did they subject us to such inhuman treatment? What crimes did those little children commit to be punished so severely?

On the firth day there was good news. Tibi had found where we were and was at the fence waiting to see us. They had let him come to say goodbye to Dad, Mom, Barna and me before shipping him out to do forced labor on the Russian front.

We raced to him only to discover that our captors would not let him past the gate into the compound. Dad and Mom pleaded over and over with the guards to let him in and be with us for a while. Their pleas were ignored. Dad promised a guard he could have anything he wanted; after the war was over my father vowed he would pay for him to go anywhere, do anything—pay him anything. Just open the gate was Dad's only request.

"Crazy man. You dreamer," smirked the guard. "You are never coming out of this hell," he gloated. "Don't you know that?"

Tibi was pleading from the other side. "Please, just let me hug my parents one last time." There was no answer. "Please, let me hand them this package—a little food for my mother and my father."

Mom broke into hysterics. Unable to get to her beloved son she came apart emotionally. Dad tried to calm her. "Don't let him remember you like this," Dad pleaded. He told her it was better than nothing. It was more than we expected when he said goodbye to us on the telephone from Debrecen.

Mom's heart-rendering cries continued. It was more than any of us could bear. In desperation I picked out the youngest of the Arrow-Cross guards, the one now left standing at the gate in the fence. I ran to him and breathlessly pleaded, "All we want is a few short minutes with him. You must have a mother. Can't you see the hurt that this is causing? It's nothing for you to open the gate. It is everything to us. But don't do it for us. Do it for God."

The guard took a long look at me. Finally he said, softly, "Okay. I will turn away. But just for a few minutes." And he let the gate swing open.

I don't know how mother made it the couple of feet to Tibi after he quickly stepped through the opening in the fence. She collapsed in front of him, sobbing. We were all crying. We were all trying to hold him at once.

Tibi gathered mother into his arms. Holding her up he kissed her wherever he could touch her. "Mommy, please don't cry," he begged. "Mommy, I'll be okay. I will write to you. Don't worry about me. I am strong and healthy. You know that Mommy. Take care of yourself. All of you. Look after one another."

Mother held desparately to Tibi's side. As if he knew his own fate and ours, too, he held on tightly. He made no move to leave. Continuing to try to assure us Tibi told us that he had heard that the war would be over soon. Then, he reasoned, we could go home.

He took out a parcel of food and tried to give it to us. Mom insisted that he keep it for himself.

Tibi told us that he had learned that we would be taken out of this camp soon. He didn't know where.

The guard, becoming impatient, came over to me and said that my brother would have to leave before the others discovered him. I asked him if he just couldn't forget that Tibi was here. We were a couple of thousand. Who would know he didn't belong here? I reasoned.

"I know," the guard snarled. "That's who knows. That's the

end of it."

My father took from his pocket the last 100 *pengo.* "Young man, there is plenty more than this for you. Just allow us a few more precious minutes."

The soldier took the money, putting it quickly into his pocket, and turned away. Dad hugged Tibi like I had never seen a father and son embrace. It was so close. It was so desperate. It was as if to prolong a goodbye they both knew was final. And, again, Tibi flooded his mother with kisses.

"Calm down, Mom, please. Don't worry about me. You have Ebi and Barna with you now. I will be next to you soon. I promise."

Tibi said that he would try to go to the wire where Grandma and our aunts were and say goodbye to them, but that he would not stay long. He didn't want to risk attracting attention to a family as close as ours. They would put us at opposite ends of the compound if they knew, he warned.

The guard who took Dad's money disappeared. In a few minutes another guard came and took my brother by the shoulder and practically threw him out of the compound. "You dirty Jew," he breathed venomously, "get over there where you belong."

My mother, screaming, reached to him as he was shoved away. Tibi waved with both arms as he moved, looking back at us with every step he took until he was out of sight.

A fortunate chance for a last goodbye had turned into another occasion for despair, ending by my brother being torn from our embrace by an armed goon. How much more sorrow could we bear?

The next morning, April 25, our tenth day at the collection camp, saw the Arrow-Cross and German SS enter the barn. Hotly they ordered us to gather our belongings and "line up for the march."

"March to where?" father asked.

The same stinging reply festered, "You'll find out when you get there."

We set out again. Now we were 3,000 instead of the 250 who had begun the walk from the temple in our town.

There were more guards than before. The vicious Arrow-Cross was everywhere. No longer were they prodding us, beating us, and humiliating us, for they were now employed to herd us like cattle to wherever the Germans commanded. Nowhere in their fascist hearts was there room for easing our pain.

The old and the children suffered the most during this trek to the gates of hell. Little ones as young as two years old had to help carry, for there was a frantic desperation to hold on to everything that might mean survival. The children would slow down only to be urged on by their mothers, "Come on, darling, keep going. Don't get behind." The plea was the same.

Again we marched past small villages and looked into blank faces of those who gathered at the roadside to stare. These, too, were without words or even a look of disapproval.

Peasant women, carrying buckets of water, passed us going the opposite direction on the main road. Children broke from the ranks. "I'm thirsty, Mommy, I'm thirsty," they sobbed, and ran toward the women carrying the buckets of water.

Immediately a guard snatched the children up by one arm and threw them back in line—but not where their mothers were. The children, terrified, shrieked.

"We know you have no heart," an infuriated mother snapped. "But have you no soul?"

As an answer the guard slapped the mother across her face.

"Tell me, mister, have you no mother, either?" the woman cried in torment and tears.

How ridiculous it sounded. "Mister," she called him. And the only sign of manhood that this 19-year-old-hoodlum could claim was the Arrow-Cross armband that he wore.

Morris Grünblatt as a Young Man

Chapter Three

The Nyiregyhaza ghetto—May 1944

In the late afternoon we arrived in Nyiregyhaza and were taken to the ghetto, the section of the city that was set aside for the Jews. In every city during the Nazi occupation, ghettos were formed for the Jews. After the few Christians that were living in the new districts were relocated, fences went up, setting the ghettos apart from the rest of the city, locking their inhabitants in. By the time that we arrived in Nyiregyhaza the ghetto was ready. Jews who were brought from other parts of the country were moved in next to the Jews who already lived there.

Apartments were assigned to newcomers, with a certain number of people per room. The distribution of the Jews was according to the individual's place in line—not according to family. The Arrow-Cross and the SS cared nothing about splitting up families. My father, sizing up the situation, took us aside and told us to stay back and mingle with people not yet assigned to a room. This would give him time to look around and figure something out so that we wouldn't be separated from each other. "I'll be right back," father said. "I promise."

"Where are you going?" Mother asked, afraid. "Don't go away now when we don't know what is going to happen."

"Just for a few minutes," father replied. "I want to look for a place where we can all be together."

That thought calmed my mother, and Dad pointed out to her that unless he scouted around, the chances of us staying together were slim. The ghetto already was overcrowded not only with local Jews but with those congregating from all over this part of the country, and all of these people would be thinking the same thing: that they must be sure and stay together with their families.

"But how can we mingle with those people that we don't even know? What about our things?" Mom questioned.

"Don't worry about them. If they are stolen, it's still better if we can stay together. The sacrifice is worth it. So please, honey, don't worry about them."

"See if you can find out where they have taken my mother," mother pleaded.

"Okay," father promised. And then he got lost in the swelling, frightening crowd.

Dad was back soon with a big grin on his face. In the past 15 minutes half the people waiting in the street had been shoved into various houses and apartments. Most were separated from their loved ones. But Dad was still smiling. He quickly told us to bring our suitcases and follow him.

Following in his steps we quickly came to a house. We did not go inside. Instead, Dad led the way up a ladder proped up against the outside of the building reaching to an outside door that opened out from an attic. After scaling the ladder we stepped through the door, one after another. Inside we were out of sight of the street, and, more importantly, there was no one in the attic but us.

"Heaven!" Dad exclaimed. He looked happier than we had seen him in days. Sensing our excitement he made a grand sweep, turning with outstretched arms to present his discovery to us—and promptly bumped his head on the ceiling, nearly falling. The attic room had a triangular pitched roof. Only in the center was there sufficient room for an adult to stand upright. Realizing this, Dad burst out laughing.

"Look, look!" Dad beamed. "This is heaven on earth. All our very own. We must be very quiet. Nobody must know about it. The guards shouldn't for sure because they'd send up some more people if they found out that there is space available here."

Dad cleaned the floor of debris, making way for a sleeping space for each of us. Excited, we unbundled our belongings and laid them out neatly around the room.

The next day was registration. All the Jews who had just arrived had to state where they had found or been assigned a room. We stated what house we were in but not what part. We were told we were free to walk around inside the ghetto compound.

My father's main concern was how to get food. If food had been available in the ghetto, you would have needed a ration card to buy it. That we had no such cards bothered my mother more than it did my father. Why worry? father reasoned. There didn't seem to be any food to buy, even with ration cards.

Later we learned that there was a black market in the ghetto, but, we often wondered between ourselves, where did those people get the money to shop there? Black market prices were enormously high. We knew some people who were getting help from the outside, like us—the police chief from home had managed to find us and was still sending in food and a little money. Others who were "somebody's Jews" did the same, but what about the rest of them?

My dad discovered a little later that we were the first family not only in town but in our district to be picked up. We had no warning, no chance to make arrangements, so they were able to take everything, but everything, from us. For those who were picked up later, by then the news had spread and they had the opportunity to hide some money and jewelry. But those who were "nobody's Jews" had no money to hide. They survived, we eventually found out, on the kindness of others more fortunate. We all had a common destiny and a common will to survive. Each in our own way looked for the means we had to preserve the gift of life. For some it was less difficult than it was for others. What we all had in equal measure, along with our fears, was a burning hope. It was the strongest of the bonds that held us together.

My father became the father figure to thousands of youngsters in the ghetto. All their own fathers were gone to the Russian front to be used as shields for the Germans against Russian bullets. Dad was a constant practical joker with the little ones and they adored him. When they became unruly, everybody went looking for Uncle Morris to help restore order.

With the teenagers father was not so successful. They, including me, were an opinionated and stubborn bunch. We had been children yesterday, scolded and treated as such, and now we were adults having the same concern for the same horrors as everyone else at the age of reason and fear.

Some boys tried to entice others to instigate, to attack the Arrow-Cross fascist guards. My father warned them that this was foolishness. "Heroes we don't need," he emphasized one day in a discussion with the young people.

"What conceivably is wrong with that?" questioned one of the youths who was doing most of the talking. He was a round-faced, dark-eyed boy.

"What is wrong is that you would be jeopardizing everybody's life. That's number one. The Germans would surely retaliate, like they did in the Warsaw ghetto. And, second, heroes usually die, as recent history shows."

What was he talking about? the boys asked.

Dad told them what he had heard the day before, from a Czechoslovakian who ran away with other Czechoslovakian Jews. Those caught were lined up next to graves where sondercommandos ordered them shot. But not all were caught. "He escaped to Hungary because he had heard there was a safe haven here. Now he thinks that he is facing the same fate as he faced in Czechoslovakia," Dad related. "But, I assured him," Dad continued proudly, "not to worry because the Hungarians are a civilized people."

All the boys and girls stared at Dad like he was crazy.

"What's the matter?" Dad asked, puzzled by their stares.

"You call this civilized?" responded the round-faced boy who had spoken earlier. "Twenty people in a room? No food, no bath, fear all around you? Where you must watch each step to avoid the mess made by children and even adults who are forced to relieve themselves in the street? This you called civilized?"

"You know why I don't laugh," the youth questioned my

father. "Because I guess I forgot how."

"Do you know, Uncle Morris, what happened last night in our building? Three Arrow-Cross came in. They were the guards from three or four blocks down, not our guards. They took the rings from everybody's fingers who had rings. And if that was not enough, they tore the eyeglasses off everybody's nose who wore them, and then threw them on the floor. With the heels of their boots they crushed every pair of glasses.

"Your civilized Hungarians did this. Uncle Morris, you are a very nice man, but a misguided one. We are doomed and you should not pretend otherwise."

The dark-haired boy with the round-face went on, talking about the night before. "While these guards were in our quarters one was shouting, 'Jews have to be finished for good,' and my mother stopped me from running over and beating the stuffing out of him."

"Your mother was wise," my father said.

"Do you think that was a wise decision on my mother's part? You mean we should just sit there and take it when they come and rob us and tell us we should be eliminated from the face of the earth?"

"Assuming you were stronger than he was," Dad said, "just assuming it – let's say you are strong than he is. And let's say you beat him up. Do you realize the consequences?"

The boy raised his hand and gestured, "Look around. What can be worse than this?"

"Oh, my friend," Dad spoke with the look of a million horrors in his eyes, "you haven't seen anything. In other countries..."

"But, Uncle Morris, don't you understand? Okay, never mind about the jewelry, but they took away those poor people's vision!" His eyes were red and his body jerked with suppressed sobs. "Those hoodlums killed those people. They should burn in hell!"

"They will, they will," my father affirmed, "but calm down please. They didn't kill anybody."

The youth paid no attention to my father's words. "Without glasses most of them are blind. How can they survive in here if they can't see?"

"Maybe they have an extra pair," my father attempted to reason with him.

"And what about those who don't have an extra pair? Those poor bastards who have nothing else to do but pray and read the Talmud all day, what will they do if they can't read the Talmud? They'll want to die."

Dad listened intently. He was touched by the compassion of a boy who was no more than 17.

"I expect a friend of mine to come here tonight," Dad said. "I will ask him to help us out and bring in some glasses for these people."

The youth just stared at my dad.

"Find out if they know the prescription of their glasses, and if they do, we will try to help them. Unfortunately I have no extra money. But if the ones who need new glasses can't afford it either, then we'll take up a collection. How do you like that?"

The boy grabbed my dad in a tight embrace and kissed him on both cheeks, like a son does a father. He exclaimed, "Oh, what a prince of a man you are!"

Everyone had a different idea it seemed, about what to do to raise money for the glasses, or whether it was a good idea in the first place. Food, they thought, was a lesser problem. Everyone was adjusting to hunger and if someone got too hungry, everyone was eager to help and make sure somehow that a little food was found. Some were eager to help with the glasses, too, but others weren't. Glasses were a luxury, they declared.

"Wait a minute! Wait a minute! What do you mean, luxury!"

"Well, maybe not. But try telling that to people with 20/20 vision."

"All we can do is try," my father vowed. "So it may not be easy for people with perfect sight to understand the need. We can try."

Clouds blocked out the moon and stars. The night could not have been blacker. Mom and Dad were asleep. They snored so loud that all I could do was lie there in our attic room, staring at nothing. While I laid there wondering what was to become of us, I heard footsteps on the ladder and froze with fear. The sounds were getting closer.

I shook my father violently. "Daddy! Daddy! somebody's coming! Please, wake up!"

He bolted up, shook his head to clear it of sleep and began asking me what the matter was when the footsteps stopped and there was a loud bang on the door.

"A moment, please," Dad called out. He groped in the dark for his pants. Mom woke up in a fright, asking what was happening. Dad told her someone was knocking.

"Or," he hesitated, "maybe it's just the wind. I'll go and see. Don't worry."

It was taking him some time to find his pants. Was it another of his small ways to delay what he knew was inevitable? Finally, he found a cigarette lighter and with that he found his pants.

Barna had jumped up by now and was at the window. "Who is it?" he demanded.

"It's me," came the answer, "Robert."

Dad turned to Mom. I could hear him let out a deep breath of relief. "It is only Robbie," he sighed.

"Oh, thank God" Mom said, speaking for all of us.

The police chief from home had brought more food and some money. I could hear the conversation.

He had heard, but it was only rumors, that preparations were being made to ship us out of the country. Asked when and where, he said he did not know. The rumor was: to Germany, to work. As soon as he heard more, he promised, he would let us know.

Meanwhile, the chief cautioned, we should collect as much non-perishable food as we could, because, he said, he was sure we would have to provide our own. He had brought a few bottles of whiskey, too, and suggested that we save it for the journey. "In other words, you think it is imminent?" Dad asked.

"Well, let me put it this way," Robert responded, "The rumor is that it is very possible. I will find out for sure as soon as I can, and then I'll let you know."

"Will they announce it to the public?" Dad questioned.

"Oh, no, they would rather not. It would distract the people, or even create a mass hysteria. That would be very foolish of them, and they know it. What I am telling you is, just in case it is not a rumor, be prepared, please."

Father spoke quietly, but firmly, "I am in your debt, and, God willing, when this is all over I will reciprocate your kindness and your help to me and to my family. But I know that your courage is not repayable. I am forever grateful to you, and I won't ever forget."

The chief told us that he could not stay long. He had to leave before the change of the guards. The group that was on duty now knew who he was, he added, and he had come on the pretense of investigating something.

"Before you go, I would like to ask you a very, very big favor," Dad sighed. We were all up and gathered around Dad and the chief now. My father cleared his throat and then asked his friend to help replace the glasses that the Arrow-Cross brutes had smashed in the other building. We all began talking at once, but I especially wanted to explain what happened. Dad told me to go ahead.

"There are these young hoodlum guards," I began. "They terrorize and beat up the old and the crippled people. I know there is nothing you can do about it, but they took those poor old and sick people's eyeglasses. They threw the glasses on the ground and then crushed them with the heels of their boots. They were laughing hysterically with their friends, and pretty soon they were grabbing everyone: old, young, sick, healthy— anyone who had glasses on, and they tore the glasses off everybody's nose."

I felt my hair stand on end. I felt a rush of blood in my veins as I talked. I wished I could somehow avenge them, and the total inability, the utter helplessness to do so only added to my fury.

"Robert, can't you put a stop to this?" Dad implored. "Can't you report what is going on to the higher authorities?"

The chief looked at my father with real pity in his face. "It is difficult. There are no rules here. Everyone is acting on his own. There are no higher authorities to report to anymore who can do anything to stop it."

He, too, was sickened by what was happening. But, the chief added, "I'll see tomorrow what I can do"—about the glasses, not the cruelty.

On a later visit the chief kept his promise, as best he could. Naturally, no one who needed glasses had a prescription, and if they had it probably wouldn't have made the outcome any different. The chief brought a selection of eyeglasses and they were distributed as best as we could manage. I doubt if they did much good, but, we had tried.

What I really wanted to do was kick those Arrow-Cross beasts in the groin—like they kicked the religious Jews, who, once they had fallen to the sidewalk were kicked some more. The religious Jews would lie on the sidewalk like wounded animals, their eyeglasses crushed beneath them, bleeding from the cuts on their hands and face. There was no possibility of resistance. The price was guaranteed death. And, as the chief informed us, the attackers were accountable to no one. They intimidated us, hurt us, and when they killed us they buried us not with a sense of guilt but with a sense of accomplishment.

I cannot shake the memory of this wholesale betrayal by so many of my countrymen, and I don't think I ever will. I went back to Hungary once, long after the war had ended. I thought new faces would make me forget. But I remembered. There were remnants, if not of the cruelty, of the indifference. A landlady in Debrecen saw me and in shock blurted, "You're alive!"

"Surprise, surprise!" I mocked and turned away.

Father told Barna and me not to go unnecessarily out of our compound or the courtyard, but staying in our building alone was torture for long periods during the day.

There was only one outhouse for our whole building, and there was no bathrooms inside the apartments. It was an old building, and the one toilet was shared by the occupants of 16 units—an impossibility even under normal circumstances. But now, with 300 people jammed into 16 units, plus us in the attic, the toilet situation was unbearable.

We younger ones sneaked into neighboring buildings' outhouses when we could, although to be caught by the people who lived there meant trouble. The young and sick who could not wait or couldn't make it to an outhouse relieved themselves outside the buildings—everywhere. The smell was hideous.

Signs were put up everywhere in the buildings giving exact times for those in each apartment to use the toilet, but the system did not work. Soon vulgar suggestions were scrawled over the signs. The least offensive graffiti read "Don't tell me - tell my ass."

We spent most of our hours in the attic. That, too, had its consequences, for each time Barna and I would leave, Mother frantically asked, "Where are you going?" The fear and despair in her voice was in itself frightening. We always assured her that we would be careful and be back shortly.

Walking the ghetto streets we saw the same scene all the time. Pitiful, broken people, men and women burying their faces in their hands, weeping for reasons that needed no explanation. Everywhere we went, everywhere we looked, every day we looked around us we witnessed unrelieved anguish. Nothing ever changed.

The young people we had become friendly with in the temple a few days earlier, with whom we had giggled over the small things of the very young, were with us again in the ghetto. Now we spoke of our youth that was vanishing before our time. We talked of the useless sacrifices we made always to please others—and for what? We wondered endlessly about our school

friends with whom we grew from children to teenagers, insepar-
able companions for years, and from them not the slightest protest. No demonstration, not even a visit to see how we were, not
even a comforting word. Only dead silence on their part, which
hurt more, much more than we wanted to show or admit.

People cannot understand today my detachment from
people who are not my family or within my kin. People cannot
understand my reluctance to form close friendships. The reason
is the desertion of those girlhood friends long ago. One would
have to go through the same hurt to understand it. I made a
solemn promise then that nobody would ever again hurt me like
that. Life, being what it is, people still do fail my expectations
of them, but I try not to expect so much that the failure, when
it comes, hits deeply with the impact of that first, indelible
betrayal.

The ghetto created lots of enemies. The slightest dissatisfac-
tion had the habit of turning to hate. In the stillness of the
night not only the cries of terror, but the hate for the perpetra-
tors intensified. Care had to be taken not to let the fear and
misery intrude on our love for one another. An excruciating
patience was necessary to avoid hurting the feelings of our
parents, to live up to their expectations. And, at times, it was
impossible to do this. They still refused to see the boundry that
divided life and death—or so we thought. It was so obvious, so
evident in every street. Those hoodlums beat their defenseless
prey mercilessly, and if it was happening before my eyes and
my father was present, as the doomed victim was gasping his
last breath in a pool of his own blood, Dad would grab my head
and turn it away forcefully, saying, "Don't look!"

How many times the scenes of brutality returns to haunt me
and I feel again the electric shock of terror sending the blood
rushing from my head, leaving me dizzy, my head held in that
turned-away position as we walk past the dying man, my neck
hurting from the pull of my father's hand. I won't look, I
promised him. But I would ask, did he still believe there was
hope?

"Precious, don't ever lose hope. It is the one thing you must hang on to," Father would say, very, very solemnly. "Without hope you have nothing."

So many times I lost at least part of it, but each word of my father remained engraved in my memory just as it is on my soul. And every time the words came to my rescue.

Besides the ever-present terror of the hoodlum guards, there was a herd of other problems as well. Although the social structure of Jewish society repressed distinctions, when it came to the ghetto, distinctions were made.

Those in the ghetto who had been its tenants all along were able to exercise a social leverage over those of us from the outside. To be able to remain in their homes with the means to sustain life, their food, their clothing, their creature comforts, gave the permanent residents advantages that set them apart from the masses of new arrivals. Besides not having been driven from their homes, they had been spared the marches, the beds of straw, and the mysteries of unknown surroundings during journeys of no discernible purpose.

Others in the ghetto diminished their miseries in other ways. They bought and sold anything they had of value. Trades were set in motion by those lucky enough to have something to trade that grew into a thriving black market. In the twenty days I was in the ghetto, I learned about the black market. Everyone did. It was a situation of learn it or die.

One could trade or buy a bed, or a better bed, or simply buy himself closer to where he wanted to get. Hungry people learned that they could stand in the sanitation line all day long, then when their turn came to use the outhouse, sell the opportunity for cash. The closer the seller progressed in line toward the outhouse, the higher his price became. Many mothers of hungry children did business in this way.

In the face of disaster, solidarity was difficult to achieve. Deep in our hearts we wished for it, and as Jews we knew of our obligations to abide by social justice and maintain respect for each other. When these obligations would break down, there were frequent reminders. "Shame on you! Here we are Jews, the same, treating one another like that."

But how could there be social justice, when survival was

many times at the expense of someone else?

Sicknesses and the danger of their spreading occurred and were made known at once in the cramped, tiny rooms. There were no husbands who could reason with hysterical wives or with the hungry mothers of equally hungry children. People, instead of trying to help, tried instead to move away from trouble, a sickness, a crying child. The sick ones had no means to get well, nor the physical strength to find food or maintain sanitary conditions. The healthy ones kept their distance from the sick ones, with the result the sick ones became isolated, often without shelter and no money to buy a space in a room. There were but one or two doctors in the whole ghetto: all able-bodied men were taken in the first labor brigade long ago.

We were trapped in the ghetto in every sense. The atheists called it bad luck. The religious called on God to help. There was danger on all sides. Just to survive, Jews took enormous chances: when they smuggled food into the ghetto, and when they brought as much as they could to be sold and traded on the black market that was forced upon us, because the punishment for large amounts and small was the same.

There was no work, no open businesses of any kind that would offer some opportunity to work. There was no means to earn one's living. Our captors were strangling us in slow agony; having taken our money, our belongings, they left us with nothing with which to obtain our daily bread.

We continually wondered, "Do they want us to starve to death?" My father claimed that was absurd. Yet it was obvious, even in the case of our family, because if not for the grace of my father's friends, we would have, like so many others, starved to death by now for sure. Our own money was gone and we had nothing to sell.

Beggars were commonplace on the streets, made up mostly of children wrapped in rags and singing religious songs or songs of mourning. Beggars stayed in a group, maybe feeling they were safer by sticking together. Who knows?

Christian passerbys would sometimes take pity on the begging children and give them a few *filler*. It was yet another source of tears to watch the little ones push and shove each other for the coins tossed their way and if they captured one, run away to their mothers, hiding the coin under the filthy rags.

After our first two weeks in the ghetto, early in May 1944, a hopeful rumor spread: Married women, no matter how young or how old, no matter how recently married, would not be deported from Hungary.

Within hours the rumor was taken as fact, and in practically every yard of every house a Huppe was set up: the canopy under which couples are married in the Jewish religion. Girls and boys, whether they had intended to marry or not, whether they knew each other or not, got together and ran to the rabbi, or whoever could marry them. Marriage ceremonies took place one every hour. Girls without boyfriends bought them, and this, too, became a flourishing business in a matter of a couple of days. While it was mostly in name only, to save the young girls from being taken away, one could see everywhere little girls paired off with old men, brought together either for a price paid by the girl's parents or as a favor to help save a life.

The rumor must have spread through the whole country, because in the midst of the marriage fever, Jassi showed up. He had searched every ghetto for me, and when he found out where I was, he asked and was granted a furlough to get married.

How I had loved Jassi, but only in my little girl way! He was eight years older and more than a foot taller than I, but I had loved him on sight when I was 12 when he came to my cousin's house in Debrecen, and I had loved him even more when he visited our farm a year ago.

I was speechless with excitement at the joy of seeing him. I kept pinching myself on the cheek to make certain I was not dreaming.

"To me, Jassi? You have come to marry me?"

"To you, my darling. Maybe they are just rumors, but I came running anyway," he responded. "Let's get to the nearest rabbi right away, because I have to go back this evening."

He wanted to see my parents. They were a couple of blocks away visiting Grandma and my aunts.

We stood on the street hugging and kissing each other constantly, overwhelmed by the joy of being together. I introduced him to everybody who passed. They all smiled and asked if we were getting married.

Jassi was eager to find my parents, as time was running out.

I suggested we wait for Dad and not take the chance of missing him. Deep in my young heart—I had turned 15 years old a few days earlier—what I really wanted was more time to kiss Jassi, which I could not, of course, do with my father present.

"How did you find me?" I asked, over and over.

"It wasn't easy, believe me. I used every influence available to me and bribed everyone I knew. I tried to get hold of your cousin Magda, but there was no answer to my letters.

"I knew that there was a big problem. I heard that they took you away from home, because the Jews of that area were the first to be taken."

He had searched other places. He had gone to his parents' home, and learned for the first time that they had been taken away. He would search for them next.

He pushed me a little away from him and held my arms out from my body. "Let me look at you," he said, and stepped back to get a complete view of me—all four feet and eleven inches.

His face softened. He came closer. "Not long ago I remember I asked you to grow up in a hurry. But, oh, my baby, I did not mean this soon—not under these circumstances."

Jassi kissed me and hugged me over and over again. He told me that he loved me and that, even though it was too soon, we must take the opportunity even if it meant only the slightest chance of reducing the danger of what may lie ahead.

"This was not my idea. I didn't mean for you to grow up so fast," he repeated.

We looked and found a place to sit down on a pile of logs between the outhouse and the very-busy Huppe in our yard. It may not have been the most romantic place for us to sit, right next to the toilet, but it was the best there was.

We sat there until Dad got home. He was as amazed as I had been and asked Jassi how he had found us.

Jassi told him, then said, bringing me closer to him, "I had to find her. I didn't want her to be taken away, so I asked for permission to get married, and thank God, they granted it to me. So here I am."

"But I don't understand," Father puzzled. "If they gave you a furlough to get married—oh, by the way, congratulations —then what are you doing here?" There was a note of sarcasm in his voice.

"I came here to marry Ebi!"

My father's look turned to anger. "They granted you permission not only to get married, but to marry my daughter?! You don't mean to tell me! How big of them! But I do not grant you that permission. I told you before, not too long ago, that I don't have a daughter old enough for you to marry, have kids, and raise a family. She is too young, for you or anybody else!"

Now it was Jassi who looked shocked and saddened. I stepped forward, still holding his hand, and looked into my father's eyes with all the maturity I could muster.

I was a big girl now, I said, big enough to decide to save myself.

"Save yourself? From what?" Dad was looking me up and down. His expression scared me.

"From taking me away."

"Nobody is going to take you separately away. They don't take girls like you away."

"But how do you know, Dad? That's what they're talking about."

"They're talking about women. They're not talking about you."

Jassi insisted that the rumors had swept almost all of Hungary and no one mentioned an age limit. My father just looked at him.

"Look, Jassi, I am grateful for your intensions to save her. Also, thank you for going to the trouble of coming here. But I still don't have a daughter old enough to get married. As I told you. That's final."

"But it would be in name only."

"I realize that. But I don't want her getting married in name only. When the time comes I want my Ebi to have a beautiful wedding at the right time in the right place."

"I am not sure anymore if there will ever be a right time and right place," Jassi retorted.

"But I do know it is not here and it is not now." Dad confirmed.

"What do you mean? Why do you look at Jassi and me with such anger?" I interjected.

"I mean exactly what I said." If anything, Dad was angrier now. To Jassi he nearly shouted, "You are telling me that we are in such dire danger? You have the nerve to tell me that you do know and that I don't know that time is running out? You are crazy!"

"That's right," Jassi snapped. "You can call me crazy for other reasons, but seeing the situation as it is, I am not crazy."

"And what is it so terrible that is going to happen to us?" Dad questioned.

"I don't know. It depends on the war—how long it will last. Much depends on that."

My dad was furious again. "Are you telling me that my fate depends on the war? That the fate of all the Jews depends on the war? That is even more crazy!"

"Look, I've been looking for Ebi for over a week. I paid left and I paid right for information leading to her. When I heard you were picked up first," Jassi exploded, "I also said this is crazy. It cannot be! That was crazy, whoever said such a thing." Jassi looked at Dad for a few seconds. Then he added quietly, "I called them crazy. Just like you're calling me crazy now."

I freed my hand from Dad's. He had been holding on to it all this time. "I'll be right back," I said resolutely.

"Where are you going?" father demanded to know.

"To look for a rabbi."

"For what?"

"Because we will get married. He wants to get back, and I want to get married."

Dad, stunned, grabbed my hand back again. "You are going nowhere."

I struggled to free my hand. I couldn't. My father was too strong. I pulled and pulled. Angry, I insisted again, "I want to get a rabbi."

"You will get *this,*" snapped dad as he slapped me across the face.

Jassi and I were shocked and speechless. Mom stopped whatever she was doing and came over and told Dad that that wasn't necessary. Yosi held me tightly and wiped my tears.

"Mr. Grünblatt," Yosi said, standing erect, looking my father in the eyes. He was a head taller than my dad. "If you weren't her father, not only would I slap you back, but I would beat the daylights out of you."

Dad ignored Jassi. Instead, he came to me, hugged me very tight, and kissed me again and again. "I'm so sorry, my baby, I didn't mean to hurt you. I don't know what came over me. I didn't mean it that way." It was the only time my father struck me.

All three of them, Mom, Dad, and Jassi, tried to console me. But I was heartbroken, not from the humiliation alone, but from Dad's refusal for me to marry, for the love I felt, and for the removal from danger I thought it would mean.

Dad again insisted that no danger would come to me, and that when the war was over, if Jassi and I still felt the same, our marriage would have his approval. But now it was out of the question.

My father went on to explain that it was clearer now what was likely to happen to us. His friend, the police chief, had said it looked as if the Germans would take us—all of us—and put us to work somewhere. This made more sense, for we could be a source of cheap labor for them.

There was no need for a marriage to save Ebi, Dad said. "What makes you think they would take a kid like this away unless they took us all?" he questioned Jassi.

"What makes you think they wouldn't?" Jassi asked.

"Because the Germans must have some human feelings left," Dad responded.

"Oh, Mr. Grünblatt, look around you," Jassi pleaded. "Do you find anything human in this place? Separated from the world? Marched at gun point out of the society of the human race? And you still expect anything humanitarian from them?"

"Just look at the penalty for leaving the ghetto," Jassi continued. "Death."

"But even if we could leave, where would we go?" Dad asked, leaving the larger question unanswered. "No home. No friends. Those harboring a Jew can also be punished. So it is not worth it to anybody to take us in, to take a chance."

Dad and Jassi agreed on one thing. Whatever was to happen, it would have to be soon. They could not keep us locked up here much longer without food and medicine. They'd be facing an epidemic if they did, and it would spread to them, too.

The air was getting to be unbreahtable in the ghetto. It was so congested. Filthy streets. No sanitation, except that one out-house per couple of hundred people. And the dilapidated old living quarters were bending under the weight of packed-in people.

I listened intently because this was the first time I had heard described what I had seen. The whole ghetto of Nyiregyhaza consisted of about six square blocks and we were 30,000 people herded in. How long can they keep us here? I pondered. I looked to Yosi and then asked the question.

"I don't know," Jassi replied. "But we may be in for some surprises. God knows there have been surprises before," he continued. "First they strip us of our homes, its contents, and then they take our money and valuables that we need to buy bread with. They scratch away our dignity, dehumanizing us as they march us endlessly from place to place, farther and farther from home and from civilized behavior. We live with the stench in our nostrils of our own human waste, which lies underfoot on the open sidewalks. Little children run barefoot and hungry, begging for food. You have to learn to swallow that food that keeps you alive while a hungry child stares you in the face."

"Hoodlums are doing it to us," father observed. He was calm now. "Farmhands with bands on their arms seem to have the absolute power to push, shove, beat and kill us. Why in God's name doesn't someone stop them? It is far beyond me," Dad sighed, his eyes cast abjectly at the ground.

By now Jassi was totally wrapped up in the conversation with Dad, almost forgetting that I was there, or what he came for. "God, I watched those children," he lamented, "with their swollen bellies made big from hunger. And their aimless movements. It is as if the hunger had damaged their minds as well."

"You see what I mean?" Jassi snapped. "Why I put no hope in the Germans? I wonder if what is happening is not precisely what they want—to starve us all to death."

"Maybe," father agreed. "But that also would have some consequences. They are not set up to dispose of all these people without the risk of an epidemic. I saw that in the war before."

Now I was hearing too much. I moved closer to Jassi, hoping they would stop this dreadful conversation, but they continued. "Bribery is the only thing that's keeping us going here," Dad acknowledged. "It is the inducement to leniency that permits food to come in illegally."

"But you have no money-printing machines," Jassi scoffed. "How long do you think the money will last? Food is sold at exorbitant prices. Hungry mothers who can't pay are screaming, 'We are all equal, we are all Jews. Share with us, please!' "

There were tears in my father's eyes as Yosi spoke.

"I can't look. I can't swallow when I see them, the mothers. And I understand how they try to blackmail. I don't blame them."

Dad explained that in our building he urged everyone to donate food, whatever little they could part with. "I have become a trader," Dad laughed.

"What do you mean?" asked Jassi.

"I trade my food that I get from my hunting friend for soap and for items that are very necessary for us. I bought two extra pillows and blankets here for us."

"You see," Dad continued, "I consider myself a very lucky man there in the attic. I am also grateful that I am with my family to take care of them. I don't want to think about what would happen to them if I were not here."

Dad sighed. "If necessary, my friend, I too would become a smuggler, a smuggler of food. And I admire those who do smuggle. Because of them we survive the ghetto. I hope to God they will be able to continue smuggling until we are sent from here.

"Each time they leave on a trip for food they go in bunches. They march together singing the songs I'm sure you know: 'Don't Ever Say You Walk the Final Road'."

"How do they get out," Jassi asked solemnly.

"Certain guards at certain hours are bribed to turn their backs. Food is taken to Christian homes bordering the ghetto. The transfer is made through the windows and across the fence.

"God bless them. Without those Christians and the young boys here who do the smuggling, we would all be dead."

Barna, who was visiting all day with his friends, sent word that he would be home (meaning the attic), soon. Jassi wanted to know if Barna was involved. "No," Dad said. "As I told you, I am lucky."

It was getting late, near the time for Jassi to board the train and return to his labor brigade. Time only for a few more minutes.

"How far away is the war?" Dad asked. We had no newspapers, and if there was a clandestine radio in the ghetto, we did not know about it. The punishment was severe for listening to radios, so those who heard any news from the outside did not admit it, even to friends.

He didn't know much about the war, either, Jassi admitted. "The problem is the same everywhere—no paper, no radio, only rumors—some too frightening to believe." He said that he and his fellow prisoners had a pact never to spread rumors because most news was bad and created panic among themselves. "We follow our instincts to survive," Jassi observed, "whether we will or not. It's like a condemned man just before his execution hanging on to the last bit of hope, the illusion, that he'll be spared. He must believe that or he could not eat or walk or sleep. This is what keeps us going as we are marched from place to place in perpetual fear."

I said that was the fear we lived with, too. Jassi told me to be sure and never go near the guards; "don't give them a chance to intimidate you," he warned.

"Don't worry," I assured him, "that I know."

Mom was serving our standard meal of hard-boiled eggs, onions and bread, when up the ladder came Barna. "Hi, Jassi!" Barna exclaimed, and immediately began flooding Jassi with questions. "When did you get here?" "How did you get permission" "How long can you stay?"

I grabbed Jassi's hand. "Come on, let me talk to you before you leave."

But Barna wouldn't stop with his questions, and I couldn't pry Jassi away. While we ate, Jassi talked and made us all laugh by apologizing for the smell of onions on his breath.

"Onions are very good for you," Jassi observed. "They make you strong and, as we know so well by now, it is the strong who survive. So let's eat onions and ignore the smell and live!"

"Onions are practically our main course every night," Jassi said. "We got used to the smell a long time ago."

Inevitably, the merry moment passed and the last words we

had with Yosi drifted back to speculation on the future. Would we, too, be shipped out to a forced labor camp? How soon would the war be over and we could return to our homes?

Even now, with all that had happened, even the most pessimistic among us did not imagine that we would never go back, never see home again.

Saying goodbye was heartbreaking for Yosi and me as we walked together to the ghetto's entrance. I cried as he went to the gate, showed his pass and turned and waved as he walked through, looking and waving as long as he was in sight, as Tibi had done when they dragged him away.

Would I ever see Yosi again, I wondered as I stood there with the tears running freely, long after he was out of sight? Would he make it through the war alive, sane, and with his health intact? Would any of us?

Chapter Four

The Boxcar—May 1944

For almost a month we were locked inside the overflowing ghetto. Father called it a prison, worse than hell, not realizing that hell had yet to come. Up to now, what he had hated most, considered the worst punishment, had been the marching in ranks. Hunger he could cope with, but the regimentation, the denial of freedom that the marching represented, was a degrading affront. Now, confined for so long in this place, the affront turned to despair.

We compared ourselves to criminal prisoners, and envied them. They could look forward to the date of their release and return to home and freedom. We couldn't. We had to wait for a war to end and how close the end was no one knew.

Well, at least once the war was over, my mother would say, the problem would be over, too. It was her traditional Jewish optimism, that God will get us through this. And when the general public finally becomes aware of what is going on, she would say, they, the people, would stop it.

How come they didn't stop it when they saw us being marched? I asked. They saw how the guards beat the children and the old who couldn't keep up. The people just stared at us, making no move to protest.

"Are these the people who will stop it?"

"Somebody will," she would answer.

Everything had its purpose, she would say. Every sentence she started with the words "Thank God." For every slight let-up in the misery, "Thank God." For every escape of the worst fate, "Thank God."

"Mom," I would ask, "what is it you are thanking God for? Why not ask him to explain why he is allowing the horror that our lives have become?"

"I thank God that we are together," she would answer, "to care for one another." She did not realize yet the reasons our fears grew daily, that the outlook became worse with each passing day, but she must have sensed it. She said that with each new problem, our devotion to each other became stronger.

Mom valued the family bond like she trusted God. She felt all ties of blood must be maintained. My mother spent time daily with Grandma and with her sister and her sister's children. And what do you have to say, my mother, about your entire family dragged from their homes and thrown in this human garbage heap?

"Thank God, we're all together."

Look at the families that are not together.

"We are though," and, "Thank God."

God and food and hope got to be the only topics of conversation, not just with mom, with all of us. Not just for ourselves, but also for others who indeed were less fortunate. The worst terror fell to the religious, bearded Jews to suffer. We pleaded with them to shave their beards off, to reduce the abuse to themselves and the danger to us as well, because just the sight of a bearded Jew aroused the insane fury of our brutal captors.

But the religious men wouldn't hear of it, more afraid of God than of their attackers' fists and bayonets. They dared to believe that the day was coming when their torment would end, and meanwhile they must not yield, even when the Arrow-Cross cut their beards to deliberately disfigure them. With the daily attacks of the Arrow-Cross getting worse for all, one day the son of the police chief arrived to see us. He had a friend with him. They carried with them a set of forged identity papers listing each of the members of our family as Christians. They were our passports out of the ghetto—or could have been.

"Thanks, but no thanks," was my father's response. "I am too well known in the region. How far could I get? Where would I go, and for how long? I can't hide and I can't go home, can't go back to my job. What would I do?"

"Just come," they implored. "We will hide you somewhere."

"I would be jeopardizing my family's safety. I won't take chances with their lives. Besides, it would be illegal. I refuse to do anything illegal."

"Then give us Ebi and Barna. Let us save them," the chief's son begged.

"I do not want my children separated from us, thank you very much. Please tell your father I am forever grateful, but I will not do anything against the law. Thank you, once again."

And so my honest and law-abiding loyal Hungarian father was the first to pack his remaining belongings when it was announced in the middle of May that the occupants of the ghetto should prepare to leave early one morning.

We lined up once again, the endless procession of women with little ones at their sides, babies in their arms, the sick, blind, and crippled, the old men and women, everyone loaded down again with belongings, gotten shabbier since the last march, bedrolls on their backs and around their necks. Everything had to be carried. At the gate it was announced that no wheelbarrows could be taken out. Pots, pans and all kitchen hardware also were not allowed. "You won't need these were you're going," the gaurds taunted, rummaging through the baggage as the people filed out the gate, throwing the disallowed items in a pile.

"Where to now, I wonder," people asked, frightened by the guards' remarks. Others said wherever it was they're taking us it will be a blessing to get away from these Arrow-Cross animals. "Anything is better than this."

Arrow-Cross and SS guards pushed and poked at us to stay in line as we walked across the city of Nyiregyhaza to the railway station. Again, cries from the old and sick who couldn't keep up, some who couldn't walk, and from mothers struggling to hang on to their screaming children.

As we marched toward the railway station, curiosity seekers again lined both sides of the street, the majority swearing at us or shouting, "Kill the Jews. Kill them all. They've got it coming to them. Let them drop dead right here."

A few were slightly kinder. "Don't be scared. It will be over soon."

Through all the streets the shouts and threats accompanied us. At the station more Germans waited. When they saw us, they broke into loud laughter, pointing to those who had piled their bedding on their backs, making an odd sight.

Bellowing with laughter, the soldiers grabbed at the bedding trying to pull it from the strings that held it tightly to the people's backs. But it wouldn't come loose right away, and the prisoners tried frantically to untie it because as the Germans pulled, not just the bedrools but the clothes they were wearing were coming off. This caused more laughter and more SS jumped in, shouting words we did not understand, and pulled their ridiculous looking prey out of line. The SS made a game, a contest, pushing the poor and degraded souls back and forth while the rest of us were kicked and shoved in front of a row of boxcars.

The boxcars had wide, sliding doors that when shut closed in the entire car except for an opening of approximately one square foot on each side, but high up, almost where the side met the ceiling. My father was horrified. "Don't tell me they are going to put us in those cattle cars!"

But before we could wonder any further, guards ordered us to put down our suitcases and keep with us only the two days' food supply that we had been ordered in the ghetto to prepare. Our suitcases would be put in another car, they told us. "Write your names on your belongings, and make sure everything is marked with big letters." Everybody got busy searching everywhere for pens, because they shouted, "Fast, fast, fast!"

It didn't occur to anyone that we would never see our baggage again. The purpose of the lie was to prevent panic.

We were thousands of people jammed together now, and those of us in the middle of the mass suddenly saw people running and shrieking up ahead. "What's the matter, what goes on there?" we frantically asked our Hungarian guards. They shrugged. They said they didn't know.

Dad pushed some money at one of them and asked where we were going. The guard looked around, stuck his hand out for the money, and said, "Wait a minute." He left and was back in a few minutes. "The shouting and crying up front are from families being separated," he said listlessly. "As the wagons are filled, members of families left over have to get in the next wagon. And you are all going to Germany to work."

Father thanked him and relaxed. He said to us, "You see, nothing to worry about. I will make sure we will sit in the same wagon, and we are going to work."

I could tell that Dad's main concern was to arrange us in line so we wouldn't be separated. As we moved forward, he could see that what the soldier had said was true. People were being shoved in the cattle cars until they were full, then the door slammed shut, and the loading continued to the next car. Dad looked worried. "Why do they have to push and shove like this?" Suddenly Dad exclaimed to my mother, frightening the three of us, "Look, Margit, look! All those people in one wagon? Look! How many are they? I already counted fifty, and more are still going in. Oh, my God!"

I kept asking, "What does that mean?"

Barna and I kept saying, "Oh, God, I don't like this."

First the sight of those cattle cars worried Dad, and worried me even more. It hadn't looked like enough cars for so many thousands of people, but now it turns out they were packing us in like sardines!

"Oh, it will probably only be for a few hours," Mother said calmly.

"But the guards said we were going to Germany! That takes more than a few hours!"

"Please, don't worry, Daddy. God is with us, and will help us. You will see," Mom assured us and herself as well.

The screaming became louder as we got closer in line. I saw two SS grab a religious Jew by his sideburns, one soldier on one side, one on the other, and pull him along like a horse and throw him into a boxcar with other bearded Jews.

A woman screamed in terror. The guards said something in German, then came back for her and grabbed her by the hair and pulled her out of line, away from her family. Still laughing, they dragged her toward the same boxcar that the religious men were being thrown in. The woman tried to resist by falling to the ground. The laughing Germans kicked her to her feet. Her children screamed, "Mommy, mommy, mommy," and ran after her. The woman reached her hand back toward them as she was pulled along, but other guards grabbed the two little ones and shoved them back in line. Others in line tried to console the children, telling them their mommy and everyone were all going to the same place and they would see her soon.

I heard the hoarse shriek of the mother as the guards, still holding her by the hair, flung her in through the cattle car door. She reappeared at the still open door again and again, pleading for her children, and each time a guard shoved her back with the side of his rifle. Finally they rolled shut the door in front of her.

My father was busy counting how many people were being

herded into each boxcar. He couldn't believe his eyes. His aim was, he said, to get behind the last to be loaded onto a car as our turn came so we would be sure of being loaded in the same car and be among the first to get on.

As he gauged the number of people in front of us, he had us step back in line one at a time, quietly so no one would notice. First he had Mother stand back and let people pass, then Barna, then me, then himself. People, unaware of the danger of being separated, asked what he was doing. He told them "it's all right," they can go on ahead.

When he was sure he had us positioned correctly, he relaxed and said we would be all right. "Thank God," Mom said.

When our turn came, just as Dad planned, we were the second family in line to board the next car to be loaded. Dad jumped up into the car and quickly took us each by the hand and helped us up. He sat us down on the straw in the front left corner, our backs against the boxcar wall, our food packets in our laps.

As people piled in after us, the space against the boxcar walls was grabbed up quickly, creating immediate quarrels: "Move over!" "I was here first." "You have no consideration for the aged."

Mothers tried to shush their children and tell them to behave, as it was going to be very crowded. People in the center of the boxcar shuffled their bottoms in the straw trying to get comfortable. They looked like hens sitting on eggs about to hatch. They tried to find leg room, tried to push against each other to make more room, but soon there was no room. They stuffed 80 people in our car before they stopped loading it.

Before they rolled the door closed and bolted it, the SS handed in a bucket and told us it was our toilet and that it would be emptied at stops along the way. "How are we expected to use it," and "What are we going to do for privacy?" everyone wanted to know. Dad told us to drink as little water as possible, so it would last longer and so we would be forced to use the bucket as little as possible.

The train moved forward, and right from the beginning of the trip the jammed together people groaned, traded insults and complained. Always when the danger of the unknown was before us, the children seemed to sense it with their non-stop crying. Mothers trying to quiet them gave up.

"Just relax," came a voice from the mass of humanity. "Probably we'll be out of here very soon. By tonight, or by early morning. Surely this can't last long."

"How do you know it can't?"

"I don't know for sure, but this is impossible. Cooping us up like this. They simply can't get away with it."

Everyone laughed. "Oh, they can't, can't they? Who's going to stop them?"

"You're crazy."

"You're crazy."

Through the small opening at the top of the car we could see that evening was falling. Already the situation was becoming worse than anything we had been put through yet. It became the twisted hope of all of us that the more unbearable our ordeal became, the more likely it was that someone would put a stop to it.

With evening came the instinct to eat, but many could not bring themselves to eat. The heat from 80 people and the stink of body odors and from the bucket, from which the lid kept falling off, made breathing almost impossible, let alone eating.

Mother gave each of us a slice of bread and an egg. No onions, Dad said. It would make the smell worse. Others echoed the idea. "Listen, everyone, no onions!"

"But I have nothing else," several voices answered back.

Because of the rattle of the train and the crying and the moaning and the cursing, but mostly because of the arguing, the noise was so loud that we could barely hear our own voices. So every time we had something to say, we shouted, not from anger, but just to be heard. Dad yelled above the din that we who could should share with those who have nothing but onions, not only because of the smell but to give them something to fill their stomachs.

Most people were kind. Most were willing to share, at least now, at the beginning.

With darkness came further edginess. Each time the train jerked, the bucket made spilling noises. People screamed, "Watch it! For God's sake, keep the lid on!"

The bucket had already reduced us all to humiliation. We had agreed earlier that grownups should use it only after dark, but some had not been able to wait. "Don't look, please don't look," they would cry. Or they would say simply, "I'm sorry." By nighttime, the bucket filled to overflowing, and the straw around it became fouled. People pulled back from it—and pressed against others who yelled, "Don't crowd! You're hurting my foot." Then the reply came, "OK, switch places with me, and I'll let *you* crowd *me*."

Finally, it quieted down a little, to the point where I could hear the annoying sound of people chewing, or rustling the straw as they tried to sleep.

Everyone became a speculator on where we were going. Why. For how long. Some said "maybe the children will be sent to school while the adults work and the old ones stay at home." "Whatever is ahead is bound to be better than this, and from what we have just come from." "So let's learn to get along with one another and get through this grief as best we can." And with that relaxing thought most of us dozed off.

In the middle of the night Dad gently shook our shoulders, waking us and telling us to be quiet and not to wake our neighbors. "I want you to go to the toilet now while everyone is sleeping, so you don't have to go in the daytime tomorrow."

He climbed over everybody, brought the almost full bucket to our corner and shielded it with his body while we used it. Just as quietly he returned it to its place when we had finished.

But someone heard and woke up. "Keep it! I don't want it anymore. You moved it. You keep it!"

"But this is where it came from and where it belongs," Dad countered.

Now dozens of people were awake, shushing and asking for quiet. "Don't shush me!" someone shouted.

"Quiet, please. Don't wake the children. Shut up!"

It took hours to calm down everybody, and by then the children started to wake up and cry for food. This woke the older people, who began to pray. It was still dark inside the boxcar and when a cigarette lighter flared up—to look for something lost in the straw—people yelled, "Put it out, put it out! God forbid, a fire should start. We will all be burned alive." A no smoking sign was posted in the boxcar—as if anyone would dare.

Morning came. Then full daylight. The train rumbled on. Everyone was more or less quiet, until about 10 o'clock when a man stood up and looked around. "Where is the wise guy who said we would be out of this mess by early morning? What happened, my friend? Did you miscalculate?"

"Shut up and sit down," several said at the same time.

The man did neither.

"You know what's going to happen?"

Nobody answered. No one wanted to hear his theories—not even if they were correct.

"Either they're going to keep us in these wagons until we die, or leave us here until we want to kill ourselves."

Immediately the elders prayed aloud as they did when in the presence of someone sick or insane.

The train stopped. At once people hammered on the walls of the cattle car for someone to come and empty the bucket.

No one came. The train moved away. It stopped again after an hour or so. Then it moved again.

At the fourth stop, the door slid open, letting in a gust of fresh air. An SS guard ordered two men to bring the bucket and get out. The men climbed down, the bucket's contents slopping over the side as they struggled with it.

"Be careful, you idiot—you moron!" some unseen voice cried out from within the car.

"You can do it better? The pleasure is all yours!"

As the men emptied the bucket, guarded by the German soldier, we filled our lungs with fresh air and wondered where we were. No one had any idea. We were just glad for the clean air and the empty bucket. My mother's "Thank God" was echoed by nearly all as the door closed and was bolted. The voyage continued.

At lunchtime the matter came up again of sharing with those who had only onions. This time fewer volunteered. And my mother pleaded with Dad for us not to share either, as, she noted, we did not know how long the trip would last and our own supplies were getting low.

The desire to stand up and stretch the legs was tremendous. Each time Dad and Mom did, whoever was sitting next to them edged over a little bit more, leaving them less space, making it harder for them to sit down.

By the end of the second day, the smell, the noise, the aching cramped-up legs brought out the intolerance in everybody, including my father. Expecting that the trip would have been over by now, those who had brought what they thought was plenty to eat had eaten and drunk too freely. Now they were down to practically nothing and had started to panic.

The bucket filled again. Ventilation was poor. The stench was back. We could barely breathe.

The drone of prayers from the religious got on the nerves of some. "Hey, you! Why do you bother praying all day long? What good is it doing you?"

One of the bearded men looked at his inquisitor. "I am praying," he answered calmly, "so that you too may get out safely from this hell. And the way you are carrying on, surely you need all the praying I can do for you."

Kids became restless. They couldn't sit any longer. They cried. They wanted to "go outside." One cry set off another and another, and the sound added to the stink and stuffiness of the packed cattle car.

The first cry automatically triggered the rest of the children. We thought we would lose our minds.

People became less tolerant of the children. "Shut up!" was the most often repeated phrase. "Shut up, you little brat, or I'll beat the pants off you," came hurled curses.

One old man couldn't take the crying next to him any longer. He turned around and slapped the child who was about five years old. Like a tiger, the mother sprang on the man, slapping and clawing at him.

The fight had broken out close to the waste bucket. Everybody screamed, "Stop! Watch out! The bucket!"

Now the old man's wife made a sudden move to protect her husband from the enraged mother. In her frustration she tipped the bucket, half full, all the way over on to its side.

Hell broke loose. Everybody nearly jumped away, falling on top of others, screaming, cursing, lunging to escape where there was no escape.

Father pleaded for calm. "Before we all smother and kill each other, let's look for a solution." He got others to help him gather enough straw to stifle some of the horrible odor. Those from whom the straw was taken for this purpose were given other straw, which was donated by us and others at Dad's patient direction until each had a little less to sit on but enough was found to covered the spilled contents.

To keep the smell from overpowering us required more and more applications of straw, and by the fourth day nobody wanted to donate anymore. The layer under us was getting thinner and our bottoms were sore. Food was down to practically nothing. A few people had only a few scraps left.

We were terribly thirsty. Our family's flask of coffee was gone. My father still had the whiskey being saved for the "unknown." We took a little of this now to wet our lips, and we passed it around to others to do the same. My mother suggested to Dad that he give some drops to the children, too. It might help them to sleep.

My father, while he had everyone's attention with the passing around of the whiskey bottle, pleaded for all to stop fighting, to try to be civilized. "We may be thrown together for a long time," Dad observed. "Enemies among ourselves is a luxury we can't afford."

A man who knew my father from before started shouting, "I am hungry, and I am thirsty, and what would you know about that, you from the kingdom of plenty? Did you ever see a ration card? Did you ever feel hunger? Do you know what it is?" He showered my father with accusations.

Father did not answer him. The man got angrier and his eyes went wild. Suddenly he stood and, without warning, unbuttoned his trousers and began to urinate into his small drinking cup. Everyone froze in shock. For a second, the car became silent, except for the rattle of its movement on the tracks. Then a woman screamed and hid her childrens' eyes with her hands. "Oh, my God, oh, my God!" the woman shouted, "Somebody, please stop that animal."

No one could stop him. There were only children within reach of him.

With a sweeping, triumphant motion, the man lifted the cup and swallowed its contents. Wiping his mouth with the back of his hand he sat down abruptly.

"Pig!" women all over the car shouted. "Animal!"

The man just grinned with a crazed look. He said calmly, "I am not thirsty anymore." He had gone mad before our eyes. His insanity stayed with him and with us for the rest of the trip.

Two old men had fallen into semiconsciousness by the fifth day. We prayed they wouldn't die before the train stopped. We continued wondering when that would be, and wondered what we would do with anyone who died. No one outside would know. Would the dead just lie there among us?

The door had not opened again after the emptying of the bucket that first and only time. The SS never came for it again. And, it was turned over many times. But, by now, the fifth day, no one cared enough to do anything about it.

People no longer used the bucket. Instead they relieved themselves next to it, and tried to cover the waste with stinking straw that had been used before.

People no longer helped one another. We fell over each other routinely and only occasionally would someone complain. "Where do you think you are? On the Orient Express?"

In our family, the biggest shock of the fifth day in the cattle car was to open our eyes that morning to discover that my father's black hair had turned snow white. The five-day growth of beard on his face was still black, but the change in his appearance left him looking tired and worn and like an old man. He had turned 49 years old just days before our awful journey had begun a month ago.

Mother, Barna and I attempted to hid our concern from him. "Are you okay, Dad?" was all we said.

Dad gestured that he was fine.

"God will help," mother promised.

"He better hurry," Dad sighed quietly.

Slowly, because the mind wants to reject that such a thing is happening, I was coming to realize that the human tragedy, whatever it was, was not confined to the unfortunate few who felt the fists and bayonets of evil guards, but was descending over all of us. How much could a human bear? The question applied to all of us now.

They had not opened our door since the first time on the afternoon of the second day. The train had stopped twice since then. Now it had stopped again. Again we banged on the door and the walls until our knuckles bled.

We heard talking and laughter outside. Dad lifted me up to the little opening to attract their attention and so I could get a little fresh air. But the space was so narrow and others pushed against him so much that he couldn't move enough to hold me high enough for me to see out.

The loud screams inside had turned to low moans from the weakness of hunger. Primitive instincts of survival overtook us. Mother had a slice of bread for each of us, but she waited until it was dark and she could slip it into our mouths in secret, so others wouldn't see.

We smelled something awful. The clothes were sticking to our bodies. Our mouths smelled. We were coming into the sixth day.

There was no longer a drop of water anywhere. The old, the sick and the children were numb and therefore quiet now. Only here and there would come the cry of an infant or child. "Mommy, I am hungry," we could hear occasionally; or, "Mommy, I am thirsty," and the mother would say, "Soon, my child, very soon."

Looking at those physically and emotionally destitute people, I wondered if we all would die here, starving among strangers in this horrible filth. I still do not understand why they did this to us, even though I have heard all the theories and explanations of the Holocaust experts. Why kill us like this? Every time I see a train go by, I am reminded of that unanswered question.

We were going backward. Hope sprang up. Maybe they are taking us home. Then we went forward again, and the fear came back.

"When are we going to be there?" I asked my mother and father.

"I wish I could tell you, my darling," Mom said. "I wish I could tell you—but surely, soon, very soon."

People in pain who had medication left at first stopped taking their pills and capsules, because the water was gone and their mouths were dry. By this sixth day, people were taking their medicines, using urine to swallow it down.

"Close your eyes, everybody." Now no one called them pigs. No one cared.

If my priorities in life greatly differ from others, the reasons began to form on that train, in that cattle wagon. The reasoning process would continue now—at another place.

Laci Grünblatt, 1940

Tibi Grünblatt, 1945

Chapter Five

Auschwitz—May 1944

We arrived outside the Auschwitz extermination camp in Poland on May 22, 1944, with joy in our hearts. Finally, fresh air! Water! We could have a drink of water now, surely. There was no doubt the dreadful, dehumanizing trip was finally over, for the train had stopped and the doors were being rolled open. Those who could still rejoice repeated over and over, "Thank God! Thank God! Fresh air! Water, where is the water?" The old ones, delirious and dehydrated, sat where they were on the foul straw in the cattle car, staring at us questioningly, their mouths open.

But those with enough life left in them smiled and laughed and clambered over one another toward the great wall of daylight that was the open door. "We're here! We're here!"

"Where?" someone asked. No one knew or cared right now, as the rush to the door became frantic.

"Be careful," my father called out. "Let's not kill each other now that the worst is over!"

We jumped down from the boxcar into a mass of jostling people. "Where are we?" "What place is this?" We looked at Dad for an answer.

"Everybody, just stay close to one another," he said, "With so many people, God forbid we should get separated."

Through the crowds of new arrivals, the other sign of life we saw was a bunch of men in uniforms of alternating blue and white stripes two inches wide. Down the middle of their close-cropped hair was a bald stripe, also about two inches wide.

"We must be in some prison," Dad said quietly. The heads and arms sticking out of the uniforms looked like skeletons. They all looked crazy to me.

"Maybe we're near an insane asylum," mother suggested.

"Could be."

Now dozens of SS arrived, more than I had ever seen together. Each one led a large German shepard dog on a leash. The SS and their dogs were walking through the middle of the crowd, getting closer to us. I couldn't figure out how the army permitted them to have their dogs with them. I asked my parents, but they did not understand it either.

The living skeletons in the striped uniforms each pulled or pushed a hand cart, into which they were placing our suitcases from the boxcar. Women called out to them, "Oh, that's mine. Please be careful."

The Germans were in amongst our group now.

"*Los! Los! Los!*" The SS shouted to the old people still laboring to get out of the cattle car.

"*Heraus! Heraus!*"

I knew this meant "get out," but my father asked Barna and me what else they were saying and what was their hurry.

Frightened, we said we didn't know.

"Four years of German you studied in school and you don't know what he's talking about?"

I knew my father was annoyed with us because he was desperate for information. But we were scared and couldn't be of any other help.

The SS shouted and grabbed people by the arms, legs, or hair. Again my father asked me, "You went to school for four years and studied German, and you don't know what they are shouting?"

"Dad, I'm sorry. I don't know."

Hearing us speaking Hungarian must have drawn the attention of the SS and made them even more angry. One of them gave me a brutal shove as he walked by with his dog. "*Los! Los!*" he kept shouting. Nobody understood. Then they started to herd us, shoving and pushing us, with their hands and guns, like animals, toward each other.

"*Schneller! Schneller!*" they shouted now, and "*Los! Los!*" By now we understood that to mean "move ... faster," it meant "hurry, hurry" because if we didn't they pushed us with their guns.

With the pushing and shoving, some children got separated from their mothers and cried. All the cattle car doors had been opened at the same time. Confusion was inevitable.

Hysterically mothers cried out the names of their children. Lost relatives also called out to each other. All along the lines of bewildered, tired travelers, little ones cried, "Mama, mama, mama."

"Where is your mama?" strangers asked the children.

"Where are my children?" mothers screamed.

A mother recognized her child's voice. She shouted, "Baby, where are you?"

"Here, mama."

"Where is 'here'? I'm coming!" But an SS guard shoved her, tearing at her hair and her clothes, back into the crowd.

Unbelievably, her child's voice was drowned out among the cries of the other children who were being picked up and thrown into the back of a big black waiting truck. One after another the screaming children were simply being thrown by soldiers into the truck until their horrified mothers were shoved back into the mass of people still gathered along the railroad tracks. The trucks were huge, open at the back, with black canvas tops. Other trucks stood by. White ones with red cross signs on the sides. The SS tried to quiet the hysteria of the crying mothers by shoving them and striking them with their rifles instead of with their fists.

The rumble of trucks was constant. People disappeared into them and were driven away only minutes after they had climbed down from the trains on which they had arrived at this place. My father said the presence of the red crosses was a sign of hope. But the brutal handling of people, especially the little ones, now joined by the elderly, being hurled into the trucks worried my father. The concern showed all over his face.

The SS thrust more and more people toward the vehicles—the old ones, the sick ones, and more children. The SS forced them with guns, faster, faster. The old stumbled, fell, pulled on one another, only to all fall in a heap and lie there until kicked to their feet. Children and babies were still being literally hurled on to the black trucks. The little ones' shrieks were ear-piercing and unbelievable.

Mother stood on tiptoe, looking in every direction with the hope maybe of seeing her mother or sister and her sister's children. "Oh, God, I hope Sarah's children are not with those," she said, pointing to the trucks.

"Don't worry," Dad tried to reassure her. "Those are the lost children."

"But I see grownups on it too...."

"Don't worry. Those are the old ones."

"But why do they throw them, Daddy?"

He said "Because it's chaos here. They are animals. They do not see. They just throw."

We had been here only a few minutes and already so much had happened, things we couldn't believe we were seeing. We were still standing at the side of our train, with our cattle car behind us and the row of trucks in front of us. My mother was trying to cover my eyes, saying, "Don't look, my child, don't look there," where the SS loaded the trucks as they had the boxcars, pushing and shoving the old and the sick and the helpless.

Children suffered the most because the SS grabbed and yanked them. Their arms and legs almost parted from their bodies.

As the SS were throwing the infants and children like excess baggage, we saw one of the children fall to the ground instead of into the truck. The witnesses to this barbarism screamed out in horror, for the sake of the child and from fear for themselves. We looked at each other in complete bewilderment, and in our hearts we knew we were doomed. It had taken but ten minutes to empty the trains.

Men were made to line up five abreast and women were forced into a separate group of five lines. As this formation began, like that of an animal a skriek came from a woman who broke from one of the women's lines. She was running and continuing her high-pitched cry, and, as she got closer, we couldn't believe our eyes. As two prisoners in stripes caught her, we recognized the crazed creature now being held by the shoulder was mother's sister. She had been trying to run to the truck to climb up after her two children. They had been suddenly jerked away from her and thrown to Grandma by the two inmates as Grandma was pushed toward the trucks. My aunt kicked and screamed, "My children! Let me to go my children!" But the inmates held on to her desperately, saving her life. They knew what we did not—that women with children were selected for instant death.

My mother wanted to run after her sister, but my father pulled her back, telling her that she would endanger her life as well as ours. "Stay here. She will be safe. Don't worry. You are going to see her once we get to our destination." That's how he tried to calm my mother.

My father, that once handsome and rugged looking man, in his tattered clothes, seven-day beard, white hair, looked much older than his 49 years. He looked like a 65-year-old man. Mom had been frightened by his appearance, but Barna and I had assured her "Once he shaves he'll be okay."

We were moving up in the lines, nearing the point where men and women were being separated. *"Los! Schnell!"* Faster. Faster. Pushing, shoving, all these thousands of people—what's the urgency? my father asked again. But now the SS with his big dog passed and pushed my father to the separation point. He turned to Barna and said, "We'd better go, son." He leaned forward to give mother and me a kiss, but with one shove they pushed him away before he could reach us.

I wanted Mom to go with the truck, because I was afraid for her that there would be more marches and hunger for those left behind, and I didn't want her to get sick. But she refused.

I implored her, "Mom, please go with the truck. It's going to be easier."

"No, my child. I want to go with you. I don't want to be separated from you."

We looked through and over the hundreds of people around us, trying to get a glimpse of my father and Barna. We did see Barna and he saw us and waved his arms, as hundreds were doing. At least we had a last look. Mother shouted, "Take care of Dad." I was sure he couldn't hear her. I said nothing.

Now that only the women remained in lines five across, cries and moans could be heard from every row. "Soon you will be with them," we told the women as they looked towards the trucks. "At least they are spared the long agonizing marches. Who knows how far we have to go? You remember the agonizing march from the ghetto, don't you?" In this way we soothed their breaking hearts.

Those funny looking skeletons in the prion stripes were pulling the piles of debris along with the suitcases off the railway cars. We could see them more clearly now as the crowds were thinning. They were walking in the same direction as we were. Some women said that they must be convicts and must have committed some terrible crimes to have been treated like that.

We tried to take in our surroundings. There wasn't much to see. There were only some red flames shooting up intermittently toward the gray skies. "Oh, look there," I whispered. "That must be some kind of factory."

"Oh, yes," another said, relieved.

"Oh yes, you see?" replied another. "They must be taking us to work there."

"Thank God," my mother said. "We won't have to work in the fields."

We marched.

We slowed down to watch those shooting flames coming out in spurts. Out of nowhere came an SS with his dog and gave me a shove with his rifle. Involuntarily I cried out. Mother grabbed my arm and pulled me close to her, not only to protect me but to make sure I didn't antagonize the guard further.

We had been walking for quite some time. Thousands were in front of us. Thousands stretched out behind us. Suddenly we were brought to a stop. We didn't know why. There wasn't anybody to ask.

We moved again. Slower. After half an hour I saw ahead of us, facing us, a tall, extremely goodlooking SS officer. He wore his uniform like a king would wear his robe and crown. He had a beautiful smile and light brown hair.

As he stood facing the women approaching him, he motioned with a white-gloved hand, either left or right. The motions were continuous and confidently fluid. It was as if he had complete mastery over his task. Where he motioned, the women in front of him went: either left or right. Nobody among the marchers realized or suspected that with each motion of his arm he was decreeing life or death.

That my life depended on one casual motion of Dr. Josef Mengele's arm is a terrifying thought, and to have been innocent of the consequences was probably, on this first occasion of Auschwitz "selection," the preferable way to face him.

We stepped out of line and stood before him one at a time. When my turn came, he looked me up and down, asked me how old I was, smiled again, and sent me to the right. Mother was next to stand in front of him. He looked her up and down. He also sent her to the right. We were together again. We had not been separated.

Six times in all I would face selection by Mengele at Auschwitz. On later occasions, I would realize the nearness of doom and with it a trick or two on how to get sent among the living one more time.

On our side we again formed five lines. We no longer had the same people with us. From all those thousands that I marched with that first time, only a handful remained.

As we were walking toward those shooting flames, we saw new trains coming. "Poor souls," we said. They didn't know what was waiting for them.

We still hadn't had or seen any water. Our lips began to stick together. "When are we going to get some water, Mom, just a sip of water?"

"Soon, soon, my child."

It took another half an hour to reach the entrance of the Auschwitz concentration camp. It was an enormous complex, and there was a sign on the main gate that translated into English: "Work shall make you free."

Here we were herded into a long building. Facing us was a long table. Behind it sat young women with triangular kerchiefs tied over almost bald heads. Some wore winter clothing. Some wore summer ones. All spoke the same language. Later we learned that their common language was Polish, which none of us understood.

The SS came in to the building with their dogs. I mused, Don't the SS ever go anywhere without those dogs? But we did not have much time to wonder about anything. The SS began at once to question who among us spoke German. Those who did were ordered to step forward, "to be interpreters," they said.

A few came forward.

We were ordered to take all our personal property to the table ahead of us, including handbags and whatever else we carried. After we put everything on the table, a girl spoke to me. I didn't know what she said, so I called the interpreter over. "What is she talking about?" I asked.

"She wants to know if you have anything else."

I shook my head no. I had nothing else.

The girl said something in Polish that I did not understand. She got very angry, jumped up from her seat, bounded over the table, and yelling in Polish she pushed her fingers into my neck, screaming, "What is that?"

She unhooked a gold chain from around my neck. It was a gift from Yosi. I cried bitterly as it was ripped off.

Immediately an SS appeared. He pushed me back toward the center of the room where the mass of people were.

SS soldiers, pushing us until all our belongings were placed on the table, now ordered us to undress completely. Nobody moved. We were a thousand people in that single room. How could we undress in front of all these people? It would be impossible; surely the interpreter misunderstood the order. What were they asking? We turned to each other for some kind of an explanation.

The SS and their dogs were circling us. Tighter and tighter our circle became. They shouted, *"Ruhe! ruhe!"* meaning "quiet"—but silencing a thousand women was not easy.

When nobody made a move to undress, they started shouting again, *"Los! los! los!"* and began to rip the clothing off of some girls. Those standing near the guards pushed themselves into the crowd, trying to get away. The dogs started jumping at us and barking savagely as the SS became increasingly angry.

Hesitantly we started to undress. *"Schnell, schnell, schnell!"* they screamed at the top of their lungs. Faster. Faster.

Stiff with fear, I folded my dress neatly and tried to put it on the windowsill. The dress kept falling off because the sill was very narrow. I did not want my clothes to get mixed up with the other people's, it would be impossible to find.

I was still laboring with the windowsill and my dress when an SS came by. He gave me a violent shove, pushing me to the floor. Without looking back, he walked on.

I looked up and asked Mother, "What's the matter with him?" and "How are we going to find our clothes again? They'll get all mixed with one another. What does he expect?"

"I don't know, my darling, I don't know what to tell you. But like everybody else, just put your clothes on the floor. But please hurry, because everybody is almost naked already, and I don't want the SS to come back to hit you again."

A thousand women between the ages of 14 and 40, all crying, cursing, deprived of their dignity—it was as bad as physical violence and pain. They have taken everything, and now this? I thought. Breaking us as human beings?

"Look! look!" I cried out to mother in a startled whisper. An SS with his rubber stick was lifting up a lady's sagging breast. Why? I couldn't help but exclaim loudly, "Oh, my God, my God!"

The dehumanizing process so far had taken about 50 minutes—longer than the SS wanted it to. So they started to shove us again.

Through the interpreter the SS told us that if we did not at once remove our remaining clothing—our panties—they would let their dogs loose to do the job. Now I knew the purpose of the dogs. Our surrender would be to SS soldiers or to the dogs. In terror, we shed the last of our dignity.

Standing totally naked, each of us tried to cover with the palms of our hands our bosoms and the pubic area. The dogs were set loose to roam into the crowd of naked women. Cries of anguish rose from women approached to close by these vicious dogs. The SS watched—and laughed.

The enormous psychological strain, along with the plain fear that overpowered me, left me in shock, as it did the rest of the women. I felt dazed and listless, and the separation from Daddy and Barna created a sense of hopelessness in me.

"Mom, why did they undress us?" I kept asking over and over again.

"I don't know, my darling." She was holding on to my arm giving me support. Because the dogs roamed among us, we were holding on to each other. I tried to cover Mom on her one side with my body, while holding the palms of my hands on my breasts.

We were standing there naked, ashamed to look up, incapable of comprehending, afraid to move because of the growling dogs with their vicious teeth showing. Some of the heavy-chested women attracted the attention of the laughing Germans, who used their SS canes or guns to push away the women's hands as they tried to cover their breasts.

We were lined up again and marched into the next room, where women like those who took our purses, were waiting for us with scissors in their hands. They were all young Polish women. One of them, as if she was mad at me, hacked unmercifully with dull shears on my beautiful black hair, pulling and pushing my head in every direction.

I didn't understand her, nor did she understand me. Her hand was hurting my neck, so I started to cry and pull my head back. That must have made her more angry, because, like a cold-blooded wild animal, she tightened her grip even more, and with a filthy rusted razor blade which she undoubtedly had used on hundreds of others before me, lunged at my head and began to shave it.

I tried to protest the strong grip on my head. She dealt a blow to my face, causing me to cry. Mother, standing next to me, jumped away from the women shaving her head and tried to come to me, but her "barber" grabbed my mother's arm and pulled her back.

"Have patience, my darling," she whispered to me.

The girl shaving me shaved my armpits in spite of the fact that there was nothing there to shave yet. And the pubic hair that I had waited for so anxiously to grow, and now it finally had appeared, she destroyed humiliatingly with that rusty razor blade. I felt anger rising in me, and looking at my mother now totally shaven like me, I felt violent desire to kill both of those girls.

Looking around us, strange-looking creatures like us were everywhere. Tall and slim, short and fat, some still pretty, some with funny shaped heads, we were all naked and bald. It was a tragic comedy. We stared at each other in wonder.

Behind every door, at the end of each line, was a new terror in this place. My knees shook. I felt the horror of the damned. Mother and I were holding on to each other tightly, both of us consumed by intolerable horror. She saw me gasping for breath each time the SS and his dog passed me by.

"Don't be scared, my darling. Don't be scared. God watches over us."

"Where, Mommy, where?" I whispered in her ear.

"You will see, my darling. You will see."

Again there was screaming, "Los! los!" and again nobody wanted to go to the next room. What more could they do to us? Voices went up, out loud, "God, what's next?" We were hungry, thirsty, naked, bald, and shaven—and we had only just arrived.

Mom and I edged back as the line moved. We waited to see what would happen to those who entered, but we heard and could see nothing.

I looked at Mom and saw her lips tremble. She was murmuring. I couldn't hear what she said. Now a new terror came over me—just looking at Mom. She saw the panic in my eyes, and quickly said, "Don't get worried, my darling."

I responded, "Mommy, please don't get sick. Please Mommy, just don't get sick."

I started to shake her. Her mouth was trembling. I still couldn't hear what she was saying. She looked at me and motioned with her eyes that I was not to worry. But I was petrified. I guessed that her fear was of what might await us in the next room. "But, please, Mom, I need you, please," I pleaded.

She looked into my eyes again and held me close to her. "Don't worry, my child, I will always watch over you. I will always be next to you. Let's not be afraid any more, okay?"

We struggled for the necessary courage to take our turn when it came to go to the room next door.

At the door we were handed a towel and a small piece of soap. Then we were ushered into a huge room with showers. How fortunate we were—we thought, not realizing that instead of water it could as well have been gas to fall on us when we opened those faucets.

Like my mother said, God watched over us. "God is everywhere," is what Mom said, repeatedly.

What a lie that was. I saw nothing of God's presence in Auschwitz. I never came face to face with God there. I sent messages to him, cries of outrage at him for the Germans, for allowing the atrocities we were subjected to, for no reason. Why was he allowing it? What's his answer? I asked these things of my mother so very often.

We were filled with the greatest joy at the exciting sound of falling water. With the palms of our hands we collected the freezing cold water and drank it in huge, loud gulps.

"You see, you see, my child? God helped us?"

We hugged and kissed each other over and over again.

We barely started to shower when we were "*los-los*ed" again to the next room.

Shivering from the freezing water, we were herded again to another room. There, from long tables, Polish girls again handed each of us a gray cotton garment, and from the next table, funny looking pointed-toed wooden shoes. I had seen those shoes as part of the Holland national costumes, but only in the movies.

I waited for, and then asked for, a bra and panty, but the girl did not understand me. Instead she pushed me in the ribs, telling me to get moving along the line. Holding on to each other, Mom and I followed the crowd to the next room. There we were told to put on the dresses and shoes. I, 4 feet 11 inches tall was issued a long dress. It reached almost to my ankles. Mother's dress was also fairly long. But some girls, as if somebody purposely had arranged it for the humiliating effect, got short dresses that barely covered half their thighs. I looked just as ridiculous.

On the left side of the front of our dresses there were numbers in five figures dyed on. This must be how we are to carry our prison numbers, we thought.

Stepping into those wooden shoes was an experience I will never forget. They were too big and fell off, or I fell down trying to stay in them.

We asked each other how we could possibly wear such things. We wondered how the Dutch people managed. We also wondered about underwear and tried asking. The interpreter came back and said a Polish girl said, "What underwear?" We should be glad we got dresses. And God knows we were, because we had stayed naked for hours, freezing and shivering.

When the first group received their dresses and joined us, we look at one another and saw ourselves as inmates of an insane asylum.

Ordered again to line up in five rows, again came the "*Los! los!*" and "*Schnell! schnell!*" and "*Ruhe! ruhe!*": go, go, hurry, hurry, and quiet, quiet. Off we marched, on to the next horror.

Walking close to mother, holding on to her hand, I whispered, "Where do you think they are taking us?"

"Don't worry, just don't worry. Don't be scared, my darling. Probably we will get something to eat now."

"Couldn't they have given us something to eat already? Why do they have to make us march again like this?"

There was no place to sit down at our next destination. "Didn't you see that?"

"Oh," I murmured, squeezing closer to Mom, freezing. It

was almost evening.

The single thought of food took over our anxieties now. It was what a thousand lips were crying for.

Soon, my mother answered to those around her in the line. "God will help, you will see." I didn't know if she was trying to convince herself or us. Weary, numb from the icy fear in our hearts, holding onto each other, mother and I walked on.

Finally we stopped in front of a light brick building. I froze again. Terror seized me. Mother pulled me closer to her. She repeated over and over, "Don't be afraid, my darling."

"I cannot help it, Mommy, I cannot help it."

"My darling," she said, holding me so close that I could barely breathe, "please, just don't panic."

The fear was near the surface in us all now, ready to spill out in a cry or a scream or a gasp. Now pandemonium had broken out again. "Oh, God, what now?" I gulped. The SS were pushing and stopping those poor souls who were standing near the front of the line. That taught me never, never, be the first in any line.

The interpreter stepped forward in the midst of a whistle blast. Everywhere there was a deadly silence under the stark sky. She told us in Hungarian, "Let's not make a sound. Let's not anger them, because they have very good news for us." We whispered how wonderful, some good news.

In a few minutes I saw four women, looking very much like us, only slimmer, and not as closely shorn as we were, come out of a building. They carried on two long 2x4 boards a big round tub filled with soup. More groups of four followed and lined up one after another, spacing themselves among us five and six rows apart. Then, from the building, emerged another group of women, self assured and rough looking. They wore some kind of an armband, a whistle dangled on a string from their necks, and each carried a stick. "Who are they?" I asked mother.

"Some kind of a guard, I think." was her reply.

They were bringing armfuls of bowls, which they put on a stand next to each tub, now set on the ground. The women with the whistles each took one of those approximately two-quart size bowls, slopped in soup from a tub, and handed the bowl to the first prisoner in line. The orders were, said the interpreter, take a few sips, hand back to the next person, then to the next, and so on to the end of the line. Make sure you leave enough for the ones at the back of the line.

The first to be handed a bowl didn't even wait for the woman doing the explaining to finish the sentence. She grabbed the bowl and started drinking like an animal. The woman behind her shoved her in the back to stop her, as there were four other girls behind her.

The first one almost fell forward from the blow, nearly dropping the bit that remained in the bowl. The female guard ran up, screaming and swearing in Polish and Yiddish, striking both of the women with her stick. While the second prisoner drank, she seemed oblivious to the blows she was getting on her back and side. As she fell forward I now grabbed the bowl which had but a few sips left for three of us standing in line. With one hand I held it to Mother's mouth, while with the other hand I guarded her from the last girl, who was now reaching for it too.

"Wait, it's my turn next," I spat angrily.

"Yes, but then nothing will be in it."

Mother pushed it to my mouth, but too late because the woman grabbed it out of my mother's hand. I grabbed it back. She was pounding on my shoulder with one hand and reaching for the bowl with the other. I was fighting for it because I still had had no sip.

She shouted in my ear, "Bitch! Give it back!"

"All right. But take one sip and leave me the other one."

She did. I was glad to get it, although it had a moldy, chemical taste.

The women in the next row over were screaming at us, too, because it turned out that our bowl was to be their bowl next. Our bowl, refilled after each row of five had drunk from it, served fifteen girls, as I counted. Later we found that the reason for the shortage of bowls was that they hadn't expected so many "guests."

When the last row of the thousand women were finished with their soup, we were ushered into the building. It was one giant room completely packed with wooden four-tiered shelves. My father had used similar shelves in the farm building to store apple crates.

The room had a terrible smell that almost choked me.

Hundreds of women started to cough. The guards blew their whistles, and yelled *"Ruhe! ruhe!"* but it was easier ordered than obeyed. To those near enough, the guard gave a rough push.

Everybody slowly climbed and crawled into their spaces above and below each other. Cries and moans grew louder as women unintentially kicked each other getting settled. Mother and I were fortunate. We got into a bottom-shelf group: in about the middle of a line of shelves, which we considered the safest space to be. There was enough air to breathe, and we were far enough from where the guards patrolled so that their sticks couldn't reach us.

"Thank God!" mother exclaimed as we climbed into our space and on to that familiar straw. We remained in that exact position for a few minutes. Exhausted, nobody moved. Nobody could move.

When everybody was in place on the shelves, the guards handed to the first prisoner in each row two blankets: one for five people in front, the other for the back five on the shelf. The minute the guard moved on, like wolves we all lunged for it. "Wait," exlaimed the woman holding the blanket. "We have to spread it on all of us."

My mother uttered one of her "Thank God"s again. We had found a treasure by being placed in the middle of the blanket.

We introduced ourselves to each other on the shelf, and promised to be careful as we moved in either direction. Indeed, we agreed, we should move at the same time and all lie in the same position, thinking that that would take up less space.

After agreeing upon how we should lie, we began discussing food. "Was that all there would be for the day, every day?"

"What was that lump in the soup?" a woman asked.

"What lump?" I questioned.

"There was something in that soup," she responded.

I countered, "When the bowl reached us there was nothing but the liquid." Only that horrible smelling and moldy liquid. The taste was awful.

Then we wondered out loud where they had trucked our families. Where were Dad and Barna, Grandma, my aunts and cousins? We guessed that they must be somewhere near us. We thought that we probably would see them tomorrow. We hoped that they didn't have to go through what we did.

Instead of just wondering, another girl—the eighth on our shelf—and I decided to go ask someone. I jumped off the shelf, after climbing over two other people, and the girl and I headed off to ask the guard where they took our families.

We went forward to where we thought we would find a guard. One of those female prisoner guards was at a door. The girl with me asked her in German where the truck took her mother and when she could see her. The guard led the girl to the open door and pointed to a small building from which we had seen flames and smoke coming out all day. The smoke had a weird smell that nobody could identify.

The girl repeated her question because the guard didn't seem to understand.

She asked again, "Can you please tell me when I can see my mother? Can you tell me where did they take them?"

"I heard you," said the guard pulling the girl to the door, almost shoving her through it. "Do you see that smoke? That's where your mother is."

The girl was translating for me so I could understand the conversation.

"What do you mean by that?" the girl probed deeper.

The guard said something briefly. My new neighbor became hysterical.

"What did she say? What is it?" I implored.

"She said my mother is burning there. All mothers are burning there." The girl was wild with fright.

My friends eyes were rolling. She was on the verge of collapsing.

I said, "Don't believe her. That woman is crazy! She is absolutely crazy! Don't believe a word! You know that's not true! You know my mother is right next to me!"

The guard asked the girl, "What did she say?" The girl told her, and like a raving maniac, the guard grabbed me and slapped me again and again in rapid succession, on one side of my face and then on the other, cursing me furiously in Polish. I tried to ward off her hands with my arm. But like an aroused wild beast she began throwing me bodily. I seemed to be flying in all directions.

Mother, hearing the commotion and realizing I wasn't next

to her, came looking for me. She saw what was happening, and, outraged and horrified, she tried to stop the woman, crying and begging at the same time, pulling on the guard's arm.

I was bleeding from my mouth, and I cried out. Mother lunged at the guard, crying and begging in her limited Yiddish, "Please, don't hurt my child any more." The guard threw me against a shelf, a bunk bed's wooden frame, and I fell.

My mother jumped in front of me, faced the woman and stretched out her arms to try to shield me with her body from the blows. Afraid and crying, my mother didn't know what more to do. Others only stood and watched.

The guard made another wild swing at me, but the blow, instead of landing on me, hit my mother. Realizing that, the guard stopped, relaxed her arms, and a total change of expression crossed her face. With a kind of sadness and sorrow, she touched my mother gently. "Oh," the guard said, "I am sorry. I really am. I didn't mean to hit you."

Her concern was real as she stroked my mother's head. She spoke in German, and asked my mother if she understood. My mother, knowing only a few words of German, nodded yes. The guard said again that she didn't mean to hurt her.

Then she spun around and like a raving maniac again, pointed at me, calling me an imbecile. She summoned the interpreter and ordered her, "Tell that idiot [meaning me] that never, never again, should she accuse me of being crazy."

The guard then addressed my mother again. "Did I hear you right, that you are her mother?" My mother nodded.

"Let me tell you something," the guard cautioned mother. "Don't you ever, ever mention that word again. Don't you ever say that you are her mother. Don't *ever* let anybody know. Do you understand that? Because there are no mothers here."

She was shouting again at me. "I don't want to know about it that she is your mother. I don't want to know about it."

Raving mad the guard pointed again out the door to the chimneys. "My mother was burned right in there!" she flung her arms in a sweeping motion. "All mothers are burned there. All! All! All!"

She waved her finger in my mother's face. "Don't you ever forget that."

Oh, God, how could anybody forget that. How could anybody forget any of this? In only one day, Mother and I had become the victims of and witnesses to terrors we never dreamed of.

I climbed back to my space on the shelf, crying. Mother stroked my bald heead, repeating "Thank God it's over."

"My darling," mother said. "Don't cry. It hurts me to see you cry."

I looked up. Talked to her. Kissed her. I promised I would never cry again. I hoped I never would.

We fell asleep, holding each other. We tried not to think about tomorrow.

It was still dark outside. Only a few dim lights were on in the room. Suddenly we were awakened by women guards walking down the line of shelves and shouting, "*Herunter! herunter!*" I didn't realize for a moment where I was. I looked around and sadly remembered.

Women climbed across me, telling Mom to get me out of the way. Others were climbing down from the shelves above, all yelling to watch out. "What's happening?" we all wanted to know.

Like lightening the news spread. We were going to be marched to the latrine. "Where?" I asked.

"To the bathroom," mother replied.

"Oh!" It was the best news I heard so far, and all the rest of us had heard, I guessed.

We formed up outside in groups of fifty, shivering in that single dress in the chilly daybreak hour. Trying to walk in the wooden shoes, I kept stepping out of them, leaving them behind.

It was still too dark to see clearly. We came to a low structure, not yet a building. It looked like a long shed and had wooden doors which suddenly were swung open. Like a tornado all the women pushed forward, trying to break ranks, whining from the same urgency, unable to hold it any longer. Inside was an enormous, very deep ditch, like a sewer, under a crosswork of wooden bars.

Sitting on those wooden bars, which were too far apart for those with smaller frames, created a horrifying fear of falling in. With our buttocks exposed for all to see, our feet dangling, I gripped those round bars that were too thick for my hands with all my strength. Mother said to be very careful and not to look down. But I couldn't help it. How on earth could anybody ignore the danger of falling to such a horrible death?

We were ordered to remain outside, where it was still dark. All we could see clearly were the watchtower lights high above, all around us. We were constantly pushed by guards to stay in the standard formation of five lines, but we somehow found ourselves standing next to different people of whom we asked the same questions: "Where are you from?" "When did you arrive?" "How long do you think we will be here?" They had the same questions for us. Sometimes we laughed as we approached each other with the same questions. We all wondered how long it would be before we saw our families.

We stood outside the latrine almost half an hour and realized everyone had finished using it some time ago. They must have other plans for us, we thought.

As we grew more restless and tried to gather in a huddle to stay warm, the guards poked and shoved at us to get back in line. These guards, or *capos* as they were called, were also inmates. They had been here a long time and spoke German fluently. They were the liaison between the SS and us, but they acted like they owned the place, and they exercised their power wherever they could.

They were pushing us around even more now and telling us to stand erect and even up our lines, because the SS were coming to take count of us to see that nobody had escaped. Escape? How could anybody escape from Auschwitz? Impossible! We were surrounded by electric fences and guarded by men with guns and dogs!

The guards said it was time for breakfast. As the sun came up, we were standing and going through the same routine as the night before. Four women brought the same tub, but this time it was filled with coffee—or something that looked like coffee. It certainly was not made of any coffee beans that we were familiar with. It tasted bitter and awful and smelled of medicine. The soup had had the same smell.

Again, bowls were handed to the first in line, but now everyone was experienced. The four behind quickly shouted, "Stop!

Hand it back!" After that it became a routine to yell at or hit whoever drank too much. Very quickly everybody learned.

There were some of us who by the second day at Auschwitz started to have our periods, and a living hell began. No underwear, nothing to wear, nothing to wash in. There was no tissue or paper of any kind, no cloth, not even rags. The rags we found later became a most precious commodity but not for this purpose, because within a week, nobody had this problem anymore as everybody stopped menstruating.

It became rumored—and the rumor was correct, we learned later—that the odd smell and taste of the soup and coffee were from chemicals that prevented menstruation and also sexual desire.

After "coffee," we remained in formation, thousands of prisoners just standing there. I was barefoot because the wooden shoes had caused sores and bruises all over my feet. At around 8 o'clock a group of SS soldiers with their vicious dogs arrived. Some were women. I had not seen SS women before. They wore immaculate uniforms and were very attractive—slim, tall, all with blonde hair in the pageboy cut and style. They carried rubber clubs, and the older women remarked later that they bet they knew what those were for. The SS spoke only with the *capos*, never with us directly.

The SS women walked along each row, counting heads like cattle. At 11 o'clock in the morning we were finally allowed to return to our barracks, where we remained inside and were given a slice of bread and a small square of margarine. That served as our lunch.

In a few days we found out we were in the prison's quarantine block. Each day there were inspections by the SS women, who removed from line and took away those who were sick or weak or complained of any ailment. We were told they were taken to the *krankenhaus*, meaning hospital, but none of them ever came back.

Every morning it was the same. Lights went on and the whistle blew, accompanied by the ear-piercing voices of the *capos*, shouting, "*Herunter! herunter!*" which we now knew meant "down, down." "*Heraus*" meant "get outside."

As we lined up under the steel black sky each morning, the

cold was terrible. Like snails curling into round balls, we hunched our shoulders and when the Germans weren't watching, we squatted on the ground, trying to warm ourselves, lips trembling. "Oh, how lucky you are," others used to tell me, because my dress covered me almost to my ankles. Mother always held me around the waist, close to her. She would reach down and gather the bottom of my dress down around my feet to protect me from the cold below. Then she would cuddle me and whisper, "Sleep, little darling."

Many times through the early hours of standing in formation, only the *capos* guarded us. The SS men and women came around between 10 and 11 o'clock, after we had been lined up for more than five hours. We found out later that this was the German version of quarantine, to see who could and who could not stand for a long period of time. Thank God, the check was for physical health and not mental, because after that train trip, we were all sick mentally.

Our official interpreter gave us news daily, most of it was bad. The *capos* were supervisors in every sense of the word, and had complete power over us. They had been at Auschwitz for more than two years, and most were Polish Jews. There were some German Jews as well.

There were also supervisors over each barracks or block. They were called *blockowas*. Their authority was restricted to the designated block, whereas the *capos* had a wider jurisdiction. Their power in the barracks was unsurpassed, except by the SS who did not enter the barracks, and the *capos* who ruled like no king known in history. They hit, beat, and shoved constantly—usually without reason or an excuse. In part this was because the *capos* and *blockowas* were jealous of the Hungarian Jews who came so much later than they, and thus they treated us as if it were our fault.

"You bastards!" one Polish blockowa would scream at us. "You were with your mothers and fathers, brothers and sisters. You were home, eating, drinking, and you dare to complain? Not a word out of any one of you do I want to hear!" She repeated this "friendly" reminder daily, often while reaching out to strike the nearest prisoner.

When we began to get used to the *Zalappel*, or roll call, and the rest of the routine, the ten girls from our shelf in the barracks formed a pact. We would stay close together in formation, never allowing anybody to come between us so we could look after one another inside and outside the barracks. But this pact didn't last. Women became ill and were taken away one by one. By the end of the week others had replaced them, brought from another barracks, perhaps from another part of the camp. The new girls didn't speak Hungarian, and animosity grew between us from the first day. They were Polish Jewish women, and they hated our guts with a passion for the same reason as the *blockowas* did: because we had had it "so good" all those years. They spoke in their language to each other across from us and next to us and above us and below us constantly.

If we should dare to engage in a conversation in Hungarian with our friends, immediately they raised their voices so much that we couldn't hear one another. They tried to take over everything around them, and they crowded us into the smaller spaces on our part of the shelf. They hit us each time we pulled a bit on the blanket. They stepped on our hands and feet purposely, as they crawled up or across us on the shelves.

In the latrine lines we always took a chance and broke away from the Poles. We feared for our lives believing that if we sat next to them in the latrine, they were capable of pushing us into the pit—without any consequences to them.

Trying to live and survive in the constant presence of those hostile women changed the course of my life forever. Given an advantage, I knew that a person will likely take it: if it means survival, I know they will. It was soon obvious that smaller prisoners were totally at the mercy of the larger ones. The strong preyed on the weak out of habit, stole a piece of bread, pushed and shoved, and if it served their purpose, kill.

We tried to avoid the Polish women but we couldn't. As mother so often said, "Somebody has to stand next to them," and it was usually us. She would tell me, "Don't pay attention to them, no matter what, just ignore them." It sounded easy, but God! they alone created hell on earth.

On the fifth day, while waiting for roll call, freezing in the gray cold morning and wondering what else could make life worse, we found out. It began to rain. Strange, but the possibility of rain and its consequences hadn't entered our minds until then. Now we would know the consequences. The rain fell on us and soaked at once through the single-thickness short-sleeved sacks we wore. I was quickly soaked, and shivering. Mother tried to shield my head with the palms of her hands. I pulled her to me, trying to protect her back. The irregular terrain with its holes of various sizes and shapes filled up with water, creating muddy puddles in which we stood and often fell into.

"How could God be so cruel?" "How could he allow the rain to fall right at this minute?" "Why is he punishing us like this?" many of us asked out loud. "Does God really have so much power" We doubted it.

My mother pleaded with me, "My darling, don't say that. You'll see. He will help us."

Those who heard my mother preaching to me daily about God and his love for us called her crazy. From then on her prayers were spoken silently, and when she spoke to me of God, mom whispered.

"Oh, Mom, don't you see? God is not helping us. We are standing here hungry, wet, and cold. Can't you understand that?"

Fear of the unknown future, worry about our families, waiting for the next dot of food to enter into our mouths, and now fear of our fellow inmates completely consumed our thinking moments. We were so frightened of the Polish girls that we laid on our bit of shelf only when necessary. We sat on the floor next to the shelves until the *blockowa* blew the whistle, meaning the lights were going out, and she screamed the customary, "*Ruhe! Ruhe!*" "Everybody sleep!" she barked, as if her order was so simple. Mother and I waited for the Polish women to fall asleep before we crept onto the shelf.

On the eighth day we stood, as usual, for roll call. Then we were given our coffee ration earlier than usual. We wondered why. Mother claimed that she knew why, "Because God heard you crying last night, and knew you were hungry," she said, "So I prayed all night."

I hugged her and kissed her and got a kiss from her. That always eased my hunger a little bit.

The SS soldiers showed up early: at 9:30 instead of 11:00. We had stood only three hours in line. That was good news in one way. But it inflicted fear in another. As the security counting began, women in the line called to Mother, "What does God have in mind for us now?" they spat sarcastically. "Did God say anything that maybe gives a clue?"

Mother looked back. She didn't answer. Instead she turned to me, and said, "See how gloomy it is out there? Any minute it will rain. And God doesn't want us to get wet again, so they are getting the roll call over with so we can go back to our barracks."

The one who called herself a recently converted atheist said to Mother, "From your mouth to God's ear." Everyone chuckled.

As soon as our group was accounted for, instead of marching us to our barracks, the guards led us in the opposite direction. Fear swept through all thousand of us. And by the time they stopped us in the front of a large, unfamiliar building, God was back in all of us. "Oh God, if we ever needed you, we need you now."

When our panic became obvious, the guards called the interpreter. We were told there was nothing to be afraid of. We were at the *entlausung*—a delousing house. We were to be sprayed with chemicals. We had no lice on us yet so we saw no purpose to what they said and we were mystified as we entered the building.

Inside the building we stepped out of our wooden shoes, slipped off our only dress and were marched three at a time to a shower. On the way, we were handed a towel, one for each group of three women. Oh, the shower was the most fantastic thing that happened to us since the first one ten days before.

We barely got wet from the water when we heard, "*Los! los!*" from the *capos*. Some women were startled by the shouts, and with the pushing and shoving of three women sharing one shower nozzle, some slipped and fell. The ones who were hurt too badly to get up were taken away, dragged by their arms and legs out of the shower room. Where they took them I don't know, but we never saw them again.

The first girl dried herself with one end of the towel. Mom had the other end. I was in the middle—or supposed to have been. But the towel was soaking wet and the guards were yelling again to get us going.

After the showers, we went to a room and stood in front of

Polish girls again. They took a big tube and sprayed us with powder, under the armpits and all over our bodies.

Back in line, we were handed a dress, but not the same one that we wore in to the building. Each new dress had a different six-figure number stamped on the front. That's how we knew we weren't getting the old dress back.

Everybody pleaded, "Please, give me a long one," but the Polish girls handed them out as they came.

I was lucky again. Mine was almost the same length as befoe. Mother got a longer one than before. We were both lucky. "Oh, what a joy! What good luck! Thank God!" my mother kept repeating.

At the next table we were handed shoes. Instead of the wooden ones, thank God, I got leather ones, but of different sizes. One was about a size 5. The other was about a size 8. Mother got a pair of men's shoes. "Anything is better than the wooden ones," my mother said. I went back and pleaded with them, "Pease, this is no good. One is too big. The small one fits, but I am stepping out of the larger one." I went back to the Polish girl, holding it in my hand. "Please," I petitioned, "take this one and give me another."

"Don't worry," she said in Yiddish, "nobody will notice." She gave me a push, but I tried to plead with her still. She ignored me, and I started to cry. The SS walked over from the side and gave me another push. Quickly I returned to my line.

"Don't cry. I'll change with you," mom offered.

"You can't," I said. "one of these is too small for you."

"Don't cry, my darling. We will fill it with straw and we will make it fit you. I will fix it. You will see."

Now washed and disinfected, smelling of insecticide, and outfitted in a clean dress and shoes, we felt at least there had been one bright spot in our existence. But SS guards found it all very amusing, especially me with my one big shoe. They laughed out loud at this pitiful looking bunch, for we must have looked like inmates from a madhouse to the SS elite.

By the exit door to which we were ordered to march stood Dr. Josef Mengele, the handsome doctor who had separated the prisoners with a motion of his arm, left or right, when we had first arrived. Upon seeing that they would be facing the charming-looking officer again, some of the women licked their fingers to stroke their eyebrows and unconsciously reached to smoothe and primp the hair that they no longer had.

This time there were quite a few SS standing next to him with papers in their hands. At the exit door, we were stopped by the guards and again each one of us had to step in front of Mengele. He was motioning again which way to go, left or right, only this time with a quick turn of his wrist instead of the floating arm movement.

While I was in the middle of the line, still some way to go to the exit, we wondered what happened because the line stopped. What was holding us back? The news raced back through the line, mouth-to-mouth: there was some kind of selection going on, at which the Polish girls in our group became silently hysterical, hugging each other, crying, wringing their hands and praying. I never saw them pray before, so this frightened us immediately. We still didn't know the danger that lurked ahead of us. The word "selection" had triggered the fear in the Polish girls, but we didn't know what it meant. Not just yet.

A few rows in front of me two women stepped forward at the same time. The SS pushed one of them back forcefully, but she insisted on going forward with the first one. An SS guard was holding back the second woman, who was struggling to get free and he slapped her front and back so hard that she was wobbling from the blows.

Mengele asked, "Are you her mother?"

She responded, "Yes, yes, yes, she is my daughter." On hearing that the SS let her go, and Mengele, with a smile on his face, flicked his wrist twice, thumb pointing left for one of the two women, pointing right for the other. They were dragged off screaming in opposite directions.

I whispered to Mother than I was going to step back in the line so that the doctor would not know that we belonged together. "Please," I whispered to her, "don't look back at me when you are in front of him. Don't look in any direction. Just look straight at him and smile."

I hugged and kissed her, whispering, "Don't worry. Just smile, Mommy, just smile." And I stepped back in line behind a couple of girls.

From fear I held my breath. I was holding my shoes in my hand since I couldn't walk in the big one. I didn't want to fall down, God forbid, in front of them. I saw that Mom had gone left. I was walking toward them, smiling from ear to ear. Mengele and the other SS took one look at me, holding one little shoe and one so big it nearly dragged the ground and let out a loud, unanimous laugh.

Mengele's upturned thumb snapped to the left. I walked quickly toward Mom.

At that time mother and I were not aware what that wrist motion meant—not just the separation we had avoided, but life or murder.

After the selection, the women on the right were ordered to climb into the big black truck that was familiar to us already with its big canvas cover and open back. They waved goodbye, smiling, while the rest of us walked toward the railroad tracks. Soon we were climbing into a cattle wagon like the ones we had come in to Auschwitz.

As we jumped into the wagon, the guards handed each of us a slice of bread with a small square of margarine on it. We were shoved in, eighty-five of us, like before, but what a difference one week had made. A week ago, hungry and thirsty, filthy but still looking human, with my Dad and Barna, we had been a family, outraged and bewildered in a strange place. Now it had all changed.

There was no room for outrage here. Nor was there room for bewilderment. We simply suggested to each other that we suck on the bread like candy, and not eat it, to make it last.

6 months after liberation

Margaret Grünblatt

Chapter Six

Boxcar to Plassow—June 1944

We did not know how long we might be in the boxcar, or how long the trip would take.

The fact that we didn't get a bucket frightened us. We only knew they were entirely capable of leaving us here longer than we could hope to endure. The constant fear of the unknown was part of our beings now, making us try to forget it, fight it, or keep turning to God.

The inner turmoil kept us on a constant merry-go-round. Sitting on the straw, 85 of us in a boxcar, was the second trip for all of us, and needed no explanation. We compared notes from the previous trip. What we discovered at this time was that we came from different parts of Hungary, Czechoslovakia, and Poland, that we all had different socio-economic and intellectual backgrounds, yet by looking at each other we couldn't tell the differences. Facing one another, we all became each other's mirrors.

The older ones usually became the spokesmen in the group. There were the smart-alecks, the know-it-alls, and the unfortunates who did not belong there, they said, because only their mother or only their father was Jewish. These were the young mothers whose children were, upon arrival at Auschwitz, taken by their mothers or by their olders sisters. In other words, they were in good hands, they thought, not realizing that all of them, sisters, mothers, children, all were sent to the gas chambers the day they got to Auschwitz.

There were also the women who tried to make a business out of everything, trading this favor and bit of comfort for that. There were the believers and the nonbelievers, arguing religion; dreamers, and the realists; those who had had everything in life before, and those who had nothing. Teachers from various levels of grades found each other. A high school teacher assumed an air of superiority over a grade school teacher. Funny, they looked the same to me. And each had exactly the same size spot of straw on the boxcar floor to sit on.

Some talked of hope. Others spoke of doom. I just watched them, studied them, and tried to picture each of them in the life they presented themselves occupying. Some, no doubt, wouldn't have considered being caught in the company of some of the others present. Yet as they sat there curled up on the straw, bald-headed, shaven, they looked identical to me. The rich and the poor, the uneducated and the intellectual, all had become the same in every sense of the word.

I knew none of the girls in the boxcar. All eight that Mom and I had shared our shelf with had become separated from us by Dr. Mengele's selection. Some had gone into the big black trucks, and, I knew now, from there into the Auschwitz gas chambers. Others had come with us on different boxcars. It had all depended on Dr. Mengele's flick of his wrist.

Mother and I sat against the boxcar wall. I had jumped in to secure a wall seat for us just like my father had done before. The girls around me complained, saying I had taken the space that was theirs. I asked, "How can it be yours? You have never been here." The ones left in the center tried everything to get us to move: threats, arguments, and promises. I didn't blame them.

Pointing to Mom, a woman who sat in front of me said, "How lucky you are."

"Why?" I asked.

"Because I see you have your mother with you."

"Oh, she's not my mother. She is my sister."

"You resemble each other."

"Lots of sisters do," I responded, nonchalantly.

Mom and I had made a solemn vow never to let anybody know that we were mother and daughter. God forbid that the Germans find out, or even a *capo*, because such knowledge would mean Mom's immediate death.

We asked among ourselves why they didn't take us to the latrine before they brought us to the boxcars. We couldn't figure it out. How would it have hurt them to let us go to the toilet before loading us on a train for what probably would be a very long trip?

Some were desperate to relieve themselves, and spoke in despair over the absence of a bucket. But everyone knew how the problem would be solved—we had been through this before —there was no room for outrage or insults. To complain was no good either. We all were familiar with these unbearable conditions from before. We all understood that, as the first women squatted to relieve themselves in the straw, it was only a question of time before each of us would be forced to do the same. We compared notes on how we had first faced up to the terrible experience of disposing of our own waste. It was interesting to hear that the problems were not the same in every boxcar. Some were lucky. They had received two cannisters instead of one. Some had been in more orderly groups than ours. Some had children, and therefore more problems. In some cars, people had died. Their corpses had been covered with straw and they used the cadavers to sit upon. Fights had broken out—until the smell drove them away—away from sitting on the dead. Relatives objected, but people overpowered them, just for the sake of creating a little more leg room.

These things had happened only a couple of weeks ago and were now told in minute detail. I listened wide-eyed and open-mouthed to one horrible episode after another, until the horror became unendurable. Mother begged a girl who was all involved reliving her experiences from the week before to stop it; living with it was bad enough. But the girl kept talking, and as she did, Mother covered my ears with her hands.

"If you think you are protecting your little sister, you are mistaken," a woman warned Mom. "The more she hears and sees, the better she will be prepared to face whatever we have to face."

Oh, God, how right they were. What I saw and learned on those boxcar trips did help me to stay alive. While the distance from Auschwitz to Plassow is not that great, for me it was a distance that cannot be necessarily measured in miles. What I learned from those 83 other people in that boxcar, their behavior and attitudes, helped me and prepared me much more than any school could have. The trip taught me the essence of survival. The journey lasted only but a few hours; the education has lasted for a lifetime.

We sat in each other's laps as the boxcar became smaller and smaller--the area needed by the improvised toilet grew larger and larger. We were determined to survive and learned to try, try, try everything. We taught ourselves that nothing must be thought impossible. I erased the word "impossible" from my vocabulary. That word alone killed a lot of friends of mine in the extermination camps that I was in. While I felt the loss each time it happened, their deaths forced on me more of a strength not to give up. Nothing is impossible, my mother would say at the darkest times when the horrors were worst. This simple belief became engraved on my mind and on my soul.

One of the girls started coughing uncontrollably, saying she just couldn't stand the smell. If the SS didn't get us out of here fast, she said, we would all die in our own waste. Mother now, as she did often, urged me to look up at the small square opening, near the uppercorner of the boxcar. "See how the fresh air is pouring in!" she exclaimed quietly, just to me. "Can't you feel it too—the fresh air pouring in? Feel the gush of air!" I looked up and saw nothing. I wanted to ask, "How can you see air coming in?" But I did feel something, a slight air movement on the side of my cheek. I could see from the corner of my eye, Mom was secretly blowing her breath on me. "Just feel the fresh air come in!" she was whispering.

These were my very first experiences with the power of suggestion. It became my mother's most powerful weapon against the atrocities we faced.

There were a handful of Polish girls, for once outnumbered by Hungarians, in the boxcar who began complaining that they didn't understand the conversation. The Hungarian talk and the Polish complaints grew louder, then louder still. The Poles were enraged and shouted, *"Chiha! chiha!"* which none of us Hungarians understood. Now all attention was on the Poles, and it seemed to occur to all the Hungarians at once: Now it's our turn to give to them what they gave to us at Auschwitz, on the shelves, in the roll call lines, by the latrine! The girls seemed to forget the smell that they had found unbearable a few minutes ago. "It's time for sweet revenge," they cried. They called out our greivances to the by now frightened Polish girls who didn't understand a single word. But our gestures and tone of voice were threatening, and the atmosphere became so menacing that some pleaded with the loudest ones to calm down; it had gone far enough. But no one heard us. The Hungarians were screaming in the faces of the Poles.

Suddenly a genius in our crowd, fearing that the pandemonium was out of hand, put two fingers in her mouth and made the sound of a whistle that we all thought came from the engine of the train. Immediately a dead silence fell over the wagon.

The whistler took her fingers out of her huge mouth and said she had heard enough. "You all went crazy! What the hell do you want from these poor Polish girls? Look how frightened they are! They are not the girls who pushed you from your shelf." She pointed to a Polish girl. "Is this the one who did it, who pushed you?"

"No," one Hungarian confessed sheepishly, "but she looks like the one who did."

Everybody laughed.

"You crazy idiot!" screamed the self-appointed leader. "Have you looked at yourself lately in the mirror? You look just like her! You moron, you!"

"Now listen, everyone. Let's be fair. There must be here at least one or two who could speak Yiddish or German, so at least we can converse with them a bit. Let's say something civilized to these poor frightened Slavs."

Everybody remained quiet, and just listened.

Then a few here and there raised their hands. "I can speak a little bit."

"I can speak a little," a second woman volunteered.

Some spoke both German and Yiddish. But all said the same thing: "I want to give them their own medicine."

When we heard that the self-appointed leader's name was Rose, the girls sitting near me said that with a name like Rose, she must speak Yiddish. "Why doesn't she speak to the Polish girls herself?" they questioned.

"Oh, come on," I said to the little group. "Let's not guess. I will ask."

Sitting I would never have been seen, so I stood up and called out, "Hey, Rose!" The leader looked to find where the voice was coming from.

I pleaded with everyone for just a minute's silence. "Just a minute, please!" I kept saying to them. Finally they let me hear my own voice.

"Where do you come from?" I asked Rose.

"From Auschwitz," she snapped back.

"Oh, I don't mean that. I mean from which town do you come from?"

Now, with some realizing what I was driving at, the boxcar became quiet. Mother pulled at my dress for me to sit down. I ignored it. She pulled harder. I resisted, and stood waiting for an answer. When she finally found me with her eyes—she was almost a head taller than I—Rose smiled and said, "Oh, sit down, you stupid ass. What are you, a smart-aleck?"

Mother and the girls around us believed she must have come from a border town between Hungary and Czechoslovakia, where all the Jewish families could speak more than one language. And Yiddish certainly was one of them. Many spoke German as well. In fact most of our interpreters were from those border towns.

Many of the girls coming from the border towns carried the stigma of the one thing Germans had not deprived the Hungarian Jews of—class distinction. Anyone not from the capital, Budapest, was considered inferior by the people from Budapest. They did then, and many from Budapest still do, call everyone else farmers, the implication being "What do they know? They are from the country!" So if you spoke many languages, you were probably from the border towns, not from Budapest, so the less said about your language abilities the better. That is the explanation, I am told. When a Hungarian is asked where he is from, he will likely say Budapest. Naturally, they only fool themselves, because like anywhere else, we have various dialects and accents according to one's province. But I am not from Budapest, as I mentioned before. After seeing and experiencing all the things that I did, I am not so sure that I would claim it even if I were from there.

Now this thing on the train went further. While we didn't understand a word of Polish, and they didn't understand any Hungarian, we branded each other as dumb and stupid. We were all looking out for our own interests at any price, and so were they. The difference was that the Polish women had become wiser to the ways of survival and faster to learn. Therefore, they were branded by us to be mean and vicious animals. We were branded by them as impudent idiots.

The Polish advantage became obvious from the day of our arrival at Auschwitz. The *capos* were Polish there. Hungarians could not be *capos*. We had just arrived there, and we were the first from Hungary. Hungarians could not become *capos* because, except for a few, we spoke only one language: Hungarian. That, we found out soon enough, was not only a disadvantage, but a disaster as well. It gave the Germans one less reason to keep us alive. The Polish Jews spoke their own language, other Slovak languages, some German and Yiddish. There were some who spoke Russian. Some who spoke a broken Hungarian. Many in the camp couldn't even recognize our language. I remember a girl from Luxembourg who was picked up and deported from Paris. She looked at me puzzled when I spoke.

Not only us, the women, had this problem. The men had it as well. But the women had an advantage over the Hungarian men, at least at first. The majority of the women were attractive and many of them were beautiful. That surely helped a great many to get an extra slice of bread, or even luxuries like a needle and thread or a string to tie the soles of shoes together. With time, of course, physical beauty vanished and everyone who lived became the same filthy, lice infected walking skeleton.

I first heard about special treatment from a girl who sat next to me in the boxcar. She said she had been at Auschwitz since the middle of 1943. She had a small sewing needle, she informed me. "Really?" I asked. "How did you keep it when we were all sprayed like animals after the shower? How did you hide it? Where did you hide it?" I had a thousand questions and she answered them.

"I hid it in my mouth," she replied.

"How lucky you were!" I sighed.

My mother commented that if I were to be issued another long dress, she would tear off the bottom and make me an improvised bra. It was early June, and we believed that we would not have to worry about covering my legs at morning roll call.

The more we relaxed the quicker the animosity quieted down. Those who were capable of speaking Yiddish began conversations with the Polish girls, who, we found out, were taken away from their homes at the end of 1942. "Oh, God!" everyone exclaimed in the boxcar. Now we understood—or thought we did.

The Polish girls told us that their parents had been killed by the *zonderkommando*. We had never heard that word before. They explained that the *zonderkommando* were a special group of soldiers that did nothing but kill civilians in occupied countries. They were set up only for this purpose. They followed the invading German armies and rounded up those to be killed in designated areas. They rounded up mostly Jews but they massacred Christians as well—some in Russia, some in France. But the majority of the victims were the Jews. The girls told how the *zonderkommando* had herded scared and horrified people to the end of the town and told them to dig. After the condemned had dug a hole wide enough or deep enough—depending on how many people there were—the soldiers told them to undress and to line up at the edge of the hole. By now the girls telling the stories were crying. Even the girl interpreting was overcome with grief as she told all of us that those who stood around there were naked, pleading and begging for their lives were mercilessly shot to death and buried in the ditches that they had dug.

The train we were part of was being pushed forward and backward all afternoon. We couldn't figure out if we were coming or going. We tried to calculate how long we had gone forward and how long backward—not that it made any difference. We just wanted to know all we could about what was happening to us.

We were full of sorrow as we heard the Polish girls' interrupted stories. Suddenly the train moved backward again. "What's the matter? Are we going forward or are we going backward?" we questioned. Not everybody was paying attention now to the Polish girls who were still talking. Some of the Hungarians said that they didn't even believe them. "Oh, it can't be. They're only looking for pity."

"They're only looking for sympathy," another conjectured.

But some offered, "You know something. I heard about this before. I'm afraid that they're telling the truth."

Most of us believed what the Polish girls said. We felt very, very sorry for giving them a hard time.

The Polish girls told us of friends who had worked at something called a crematorium. One of the friends had recognized his parents in a newly arrived group from the Polish ghettos. He knew that they were being marched to what he said was a gas chamber, and he tried to shove them out of line. The SS all around them watched the drama unfold from the sidelines. The parents were happy to see their son and got very excited.

To prevent mass panic, the SS shot the old couple on the spot. The son survived because the SS thought he was just trying to restore order there. They did not know he had been trying to save his own parents.

They collected bits of information, they said, while standing in the line at the *entlausung*. They all came from the same town and always sought each other out when they had a chance at *entlausung* time, which was every two weeks.

"Where were your men?" we asked. They never saw them. They only heard stories. They said they were there, and they had various jobs, but that they had been isolated and had not seen them.

We realized that not only our barracks of 1000 women were on our way to a destination unknown. There were old-timers in the boxcars as well. In fact, we were quite a few thousand, they told us.

They had millions of questions for us, too. "How long ago were you taken from your home," they inquired. "How far was the war?" "What did we hear from the Americans? Are they coming?"

We had no idea, we replied.

They said to brace ourselves, because the dead had lain around them and between them every moment of their existence following the German occupation. They told us that only 48 girls remained alive out of the 1000 that they shared their barracks with in the previous camp.

"How come?"

"What happened?"

"Selection," they said very simply.

"What has that to do with it?"

The Polish girls looked at us with disbelief. "What do you think a selection is? One remains alive, like we just did."

"Wait! wait! wait!" we shouted. "And what happens to the other ones?"

"The same thing that happened to your mothers and your fathers," the Polish girls declared. "First they walk into the gas chambers, and after they die there, they put them in the crematory. They burn their bones. That was the flame you saw. That was the smell you could not identify."

For a few minutes, even the nonbelievers remained silent.

Not a single comment on the horror we had just been told stirred anyone—at that moment. Then, as if somebody gave a signal, all at once, eighty some desperate souls let loose a long, piercing shriek.

Chapter Seven

Plassow—June 1944

It was later in the afternoon when the train stopped and the SS rolled back the door on our boxcar. They herded us out in a hurry, crying *"Los, los!"* and *"schnell, schnell,"* over and over. Somehow they were always in a hurry.

Lining up in five rows again, we began to march toward another concentration camp. It was called Plassow.

We saw the high security tower from far away. It was filled with SS soldiers and their rifles and machine guns. Getting closer, we saw an enormously high wire fence attached to electric poles that told us that we were close to another prison. At Auschwitz I was scared and didn't notice those wires, so this was new to me.

Soon we were standing on a big field in the center of a large complex of buildings. The complex looked like a planned development.

We had no idea why they *"Los-los*ed" us, hitting us with their sticks. We had been hurried here and now we just stood for hours. Around us stood other people, thousands and thousands. The SS finally moved us forward and we began marching toward a row of barracks. We had the idea that it might be some kind of a public place. If not for those high fences and guard towers, it might have looked like one.

I saw men walking around in those striped uniforms, bald and skinny, looking like living skeletons. Their big eyes bulged out of their skulls. It was a weird and scary sight.

We had seen these emaciated prisoners when we had arrived at Auschwitz. At Plassow no guards walked with them. It appeared that they could walk freely within the electric fences.

By early evening a line of men and women appeared carrying soup as it had been in Auschwitz: in tubs slung between two poles. The carriers stopped along the rows and we saw that these, too, both male and female, looked like skeletons, more dead than alive. We wondered how they carried those big, big tubs.

There were thousands of males in groups of five rows, and thousands of women's rows. Roll call here began at 5:30 in the morning and was repeated in the evening, every day, rain or shine.

The women prisoners wore street clothes of every type. Some wore elegant dresses and wooden shoes, some wore cotton dresses and tall boots, and they had a scarf tied across a couple of months of fuzz on their skulls. What a pitiful sight they were.

Looking at them, I wondered where they came from, how long they had been there, and how long it would be before I looked like them. I tried to push the thought out of my mind because deep in my heart I didn't want to believe that I would ever look like that.

We were terribly exhausted. We had been up since 5:30, then crammed into a boxcar, then marched here. We were thirsty, hungry, and desperately in need of a latrine.

The other inmates got their soup and were counted and marched back to their barracks. We were left standing there. We got no food.

The problem was space, we gathered. They didn't know where to put us. Finally, late in the evening, they herded us into barracks similar to the ones in Auschwitz. At the door stood a *Blockowa* with a couple of helpers and one SS woman.

Inside the barracks were the familiar four layers of shelves. My mother and I landed on the top, which was a terrible place to be, because climbing up and down in such packed quarters was a constant problem and we were pushed and shoved with every move.

There were lots of inmates there already. They just filled us in where the weekly selection had created vacancies. Naturally, we did not know that then. We were just happy to be able to rest.

The entire trainload of us was scattered around the camp. Wherever there was an empty space they shoved us in. Everything went in the most disorderly fashion and nobody seemed to know what to do, because wherever they pushed us, the space was already taken. With instructions given in every language but Hungarian, they would shove a woman into a space not realizing that someone was already there. Here we were, five girls to a shelf. That prompted Mom to say, again, "Thank God for that."

"How can you thank God for anything here?" It was the old discussion again.

"First, that we finally got settled and don't have to stand in line any more..." mother responded, lifting her tired arm and pointing outside. Her voice drifted off into a void.

"You said first—what's the second?"

"That we are here, only you and I alone on this shelf, and hopefully we can stay that way."

"Come on," I protested. "You don't think we'll have this shelf all to ourselves for long, do you?"

"Maybe," she said. "Maybe."

We positioned ourselves at the first and second place. Mom took the first slot. I lay right behind her in the second—up high on the gloomy and barren fourth layer, high above the convenience of the layers below.

Mom pulled some additional straw from the back to make a thicker layer under us. It smelled horrible. Nauseated, I declared that I'd rather lay on the bare wood.

"You will get used to the smell," Mom prophesied. "You will see. Tomorrow you won't even smell it. You won't even know it. And, at least, you won't feel this hard wood." She continued talking as she gathered all the straw she could, setting down each layer of straw, securing it with her knee and arm, then putting another layer, then another layer, pushing it and stuffing it to make it firm. She used not only all the stinking and dirty straw from three empty spaces on the shelf, but added more from her own space.

"Wait a minute, Mom," I exclaimed. "Just a minute. I have enough."

"Sh-sh, sh-sh," she put a finger to my lips. "Don't say 'Mom'. Somebody will hear us here."

"Oh! I have such a hard time staying on guard all the time," I repented. "Calling your mother something else is awkward and almost impossible." I had no other word, no other choice but just to call Mom "you."

"Let's practice," Mom suggested. "Find something that's easy." She was pulling more straw as she talked. She was still piling it up while she tried to take my attention away from what she was doing by talking to me.

"The only reason I call you 'you' is because that's the easiest and least confusing," I said.

She said, "That's all right. That's the easiest to remember. No names. Just 'you'."

"And please, you do the same," I said, "because 'sweetheart' and 'darling' and 'my child' and 'life of mine' and all the endearing words will give you away immediately. So please, Mom, restrain yourself."

She pulled me close to her, hugging and kissing me all over. It was as if she felt threatened that she would never see me again. Then she ordered me to lie on the bed, pointing to her creation. I pulled back, "Oh! no you don't. You lie on it!"

A kind of bewilderment came over her face, a look of disbelief. "You don't think I made this for myself?" Mom gasped. "Come on. Lie on it immediately!"

"You're acting more like a 'mother' than a 'you' like you're supposed to be," I pointed out.

We started smiling. I told her, "You really didn't think that I would let you sleep there in the first place, did you?" I was serious now.

"Why not?"

"You didn't think for one minute that I would let you be nearest the outside, did you? They will be climbing up and down there, stepping on your hand and all over you when they are going up or down for roll call, or coffee time, or latrine calls or whatever calls we may have. I will not let you sleep there."

She saw that I was determined. She almost started to cry, admitting that this was precisely the reason she took that first space.

"Then why did you let me make this bed?" she asked—at which, with all the rocking back and forth on the shelves below, the bed fell apart and flattened out to a form of nothing but a black, smelly pile. Tears fell.

"That's okay," I said, hugging and kissing her. I told her I couldn't keep all that straw anyway, because if not tonight, then tomorrow night, the SS were certain to fill up the empty slots.

Mom reached for the remains of the blanket. A complete blanket it surely wasn't. It was worn thin as an umbrella and it smelled filthy, like a latrine. "Oh, my God!" I cried in despair —but it was an opportunity not to be passed up.

"You see! You see!" Mom gloated. "Thank God it is all ours!"

Looking from our shelf, I saw several women standing around the *blockowa*. I thought, there goes our blanket. I was right. We got three Polish girls who had come on our train but not in our boxcar. The rest of the 85 girls in our boxcar got scattered among a thousand girls in the barracks. Near us I recognized only a few. The leader, Rose, I met much later, but the others I never saw again.

The three Polish girls climbed up without any difficulty, said something in Polish, then in Yiddish, then in German, and when we didn't answer, one of the Polish girls said, "Oh, Hungarians!" with some disgust.

Mother tried to speak to them using her few words of Yiddish, but communication with them was difficult. With our hands and eyes, we somehow managed.

The girls took the straw by one hand, and held their noses with the other, arranging their spaces. They reached for their part of the blanket, and, like hatching hens, dug themselves into the straw, cursing the girls before them for making the place stink.

I don't know if it was the hunger or the height or the smell, but I got dizzy just looking down. Mother sat back, both legs pulled up, her head resting on her knees. She was murmuring.

"*Hé, mi baj van?*" I asked, scared: "Hey, what's the matter with you?"

"*Semmi, én csak hálát adok a jó Istennek.*" ("Nothing, I just thank God.")

"*És miért?*"("For what?") I was losing my patience with the conversation.

"*Azért mert itt fönt vagyunk?*" ("For being up here.")

"Here? Up on these cursed shelves? This is the worst!" I screamed. "Don't include me in your thanks!"

But mother had found something good again. "You see, nobody is above us constantly making disturbing noises like before. Nobody is climbing over us to get down. Don't you think this is a blessing?"

Yes. What a blessing—provided that we would never have to climb down ourselves to go anywhere.

There were hundreds and hundreds of girls lying on the

shelves everywhere. Between them, wherever another body would fit, the SS women and *blockowas* shoved in a non-stop line of newcomers.

Row after row of strange looking skulls on skeleton bodies filled the barracks. There were skulls with different color fuzz, and with large eyes bulging out of their skinny faces, staring as if we were the odd ones. With their skinny arms and bony fingers, they reached out toward us to get our attention and ask us questions, mostly what country we came from. "Oh, God!" we newcomers exclaimed. We thought, they must have been here a very, very long time to look like that.

In great noise and confusion, girls kept coming. There were cries of pain as arms and legs were stepped on and hurt by climbers up and down, again and again. In this Tower of Babel there could not have been greater chaos.

There were no interpreters, as they too rushed to secure spaces for themselves. The SS women and the *blockowa* screamed for German-speaking girls to step forward, but few did.

"You can't all be that dumb!" the German screamed.

Finally everybody got placed. We were ordered, "stay put," and instructed not to get out or off of the shelves until we were told to do so. There would be no soup, we were then informed, because it had taken too long to place us. Every morning, the German droned on, after roll call we would be put to work. Then, draconically, she asked, "Any questions?"

"Yes!" hundreds of voices shouted. We had a million questions.

First, "Where are we?"

"In Plassow" the guards said. This did not mean much to the Hungarians. It did mean a great deal to the Polish girls. They knew where they were in Poland—near the city of Krakow.

Anything else we wanted to know we would find out in due time, the Germans said. Also, they said, if we follow orders we would have nothing to fear. By now we knew this deceit when we heard it.

"Those wishing to go to the latrine will be taken," our captors claimed, "in sections, according to rows." What welcomed news that was.

As in Auschwitz, we walked in groups to a barracks that looked like any other barracks from the outside. But inside it was identical to what we had in Auschwitz—only bigger. On two wooden bars, 20 women at a time could sit to use the facility, holding on for dear life hoping not to fall into the cess pool. It was the same horrible experience again. It was the same necessary evil.

Ushered back to the barracks and our individual space, the lights were switched off. The buzzing of voices continued. For a thousand girls to be shut up at once as we had been ordered was not possible. The shrieking whistle blows were followed by the shouting of many *blockowas* for "Quiet! quiet! quiet!" Then our guards switched the lights back on and shouted some more.

"You imbeciles, you animals!" one of them screamed. "I try to be nice to you, but that won't work, it looks like to me! It won't be possible." And she struck with her rubber stick at the girls on the lower shelves in front of her. Those poor girls! They might be first for morning coffee, or for the latrine call, but the price they had to pay! The daily routine with the *blockowa* striking out with every word she uttered canceled every advantage the girls had.

Early in the morning, as at Auschwitz, we rose to the whistle blows and "*Herunter! herunter* – down, down!" There was a system here. The bottom rows went first. Lined up they were handed an aluminum cup filled with coffee. They had to drink it fast because the next row had been hurried out and was already waiting in line for the empty cup.

The coffee was cold, so there was no problem in drinking it fast. When we were done, "*Schnell, schnell, schnell,*" pulsed from the throats of our captors, ordering us to form lines, five abreast, and march to the same large field where we were taken the day before on our arrival.

This time I saw more, as early in the morning everybody marched from every direction, from every barracks, as far as the eye could see. God, there must be a million people here, we thought. Some groups of five lines were made up of men who looked like those living skeletons who took our suitcases when we arrived at Auschwitz. In other groups marching to the field, men wore civilian clothes, with caps on their heads. Above the prison number they had different colored triangles sewn on their jackets. These men were not as skeletal looking as the others. Because of their clothes and because they did not look like living skeletons, there was a ray of hope. We got excited and thought they were the men from our original group from home. Mom immediately thought of Dad, and said, "Look, look, look around. Maybe we'll see Barna or Dad."

In other rows of fives, men marched, some in striped prison garb, some as civilians, but all had armbands on. They were all *capos*. These *capos* were like guards or supervisors for every department, and there were hundreds of them. Then, also in the rows five abreast, came the women *capos*, many also in colored clothing, some of them in high boots. We watched and wondered, Where are these people coming from? Who are they? They all marched as if they were in some kind of a parade.

I found out later those colorful clothes were garments that were confiscated from us on our first arrival, from our hand bundles and from the suitcases. Apparently the SS distributed those clothes in all camps. The gray prison sacks that we wore with the numbers on them were given to those who were being prepared to be transported to other camps. All this we realized only much later.

We stood there until about 8 in the morning. Then a large group of SS men with their dogs, and a large group of SS women, came by. The SS women looked hand-picked. All were tall, slim blondes with light eyes and light eyebrows—and with the same pageboy hairstyle. They lined up in front of us and in a bored fashion marched up and down between the lines, counting out loud. If somebody was a bit out of line, the SS blondes gave a push to the person without saying a word to get her back in line. This was every morning and every night. It was a routine that we quickly became familiar with. The dogs were used by the SS men at the roll call when they wanted to give a stronger push than just the man's punch to straighten the lines.

Within seconds at this place, I noticed everything I could change. One minute living skeletons by the thousands were coming or going. I also found out very quickly that the next minute the skeletons were gone and in their place were civilian-clothed men in fairly good physical condition. Those, we learned, were political prisoners from the occupied countries—and they were all Christians. That's why, instead of the yellow star, they wore only the triangles on their vests. The color of the triangle designated either the country the prisoner was from or the degree or nature of his crime. None were from Hungary. None were Jews. That explained why they weren't living skeletons. They got somewhat better food than the Jews.

After the roll call that first morning, we were marched in the opposite direction from our barracks, apparently to work. We walked alongside another group of inmates who had been there for years. They whispered to us the question that everybody asked us, "Where are you from?" The reason the prisoners asked that of newcomers was to find out if they were from the same town and perhaps get some news of relatives. And we asked the same question, wording it "Are there any Hungarians among you?" They shook their heads, no. Nobody seemed to know anything about us. We were the first Hungarians wherever we went.

We were marched to a far end of the camp where a giant mound of rocks was piled up. We were told our job was to hand-carry each stone to another location, about a quarter of a mile away—and to make a new pile there.

The rocks were very heavy. Everybody tried to find the smallest ones to carry. Soon nothing was left but the great big ones. These were carried by two or even three girls at once. A disagreement developed over who would walk forward and who would walk backward while lugging the larger stones. Walking that way was difficult, even without the burden of the rocks. The terrain was dangerously rough, uphill over a dirt road covered with tiny rocks and broken glass discarded by the Germans.

We cried, cursed and shouted, "Watch out!" to each other as we struggled with our burden. When weight became too much, we let go—and cried out in agony as we fell down ourselves. The rocks would get loose and roll under our feet, sometimes bowling us over, too. "Let go! Let go!" we cried out to each other, trying not to get hurt any more than we already were.

When the rocks we dropped started to roll, we didn't know what to do. We yelled for the girls below to jump for safety. They would fall with their rocks on top of each other, screaming and cursing in different languages. We helped one another to stand up again, working quickly before the *capos* could get to those who went down and beat them with clubs mercilessly.

Mother filled my left shoe, the one that fit like a canoe,

with straw, but I still stepped out of it with almost every step. Before, I had carried it in my hand, but now I had to carry the rocks and I couldn't carry both and I couldn't take the shoe off and leave it because someone would steal it. Standing in the roll calls I could go barefoot, but not here. I struggled, dragging the big shoe and the little shoe as I worked.

When we walked from one place to the next without the *capos* walking with us, we were sometimes able to exchange a few whispered words. If prisoners walked in the same direction, they would talk if they could understand one another. But if a *capo* noticed, or if the SS noticed our conversations, it would mean death or serious injury. That was the purpose of the dogs.

The *capos* had much more liberty than the rest of us, and once we befriended a couple, we considered ourselves lucky. It meant one less *capo* to beat us or frighten us.

Our *capos* at the rock quarry were all men and all wore triangles on their clothes. One day I saw one of them watching me, just as I had hid my big shoe behind a rock. He walked toward me. Mother whispered, "Don't get scared. He is smiling. Don't get scared." Her warning was important as fear was our only feeling toward the *capos*.

The *capo* that came towards me was a tall blond man somewhere in his early 30s. He looked Swedish or of some other Scandinavian origin. I looked up at him, waiting, as he stood in front of me. He asked if I spoke German. I shook my head no. Still smiling, he walked away.

"You see, there is nothing to get scared of," Mom said. "Don't ever get scared. You see? There's nothing to worry about. When they approach you, just smile at them, and then you are assured they won't hurt you. Okay?"

I said "Okay," but it didn't necessarily always work that way.

On the next trip with a rock in hand the same *capo* came over to us again. This time he brought with him a girl who had been carrying lumber. The *capo* spoke to the girl and she asked where I came from. She spoke with a Hungarian accent. I found out that she was a Czechoslovakian girl who had been there for about a year and a half. Using the girl as an interpreter, I told the *capo* that I came from Hungary.

"The Germans are so far east, already?" the *capo* asked.

I said, "They came in March."

He ran his fingers across my almost freshly shaven head, and pulled out a slice of bread from under his jacket. He handed it to me. I stood there mesmerized. He mumbled something and then walked away.

Whatever he mumbled I couldn't understand, and even if I could have understood him, I couldn't remember because I was in a state of shock. Mother and I looked at each other, and from a force of habit she exclaimed, "Oh, thank God! You see! You see! You don't ever have to be afraid of them."

We took little crumbs out of the bread to make it last. Holding a rock and the bread in the palm of my hand the bread got flattened like a board. Seeing it flattened, mother and I decided to eat it up—but the joy and the excitement it created remained with me the rest of my life.

Each day at lunch we lined up for our slice of bread and a tiny square of margarine. In the evening we lined up at the center of the field for roll call. One and a half hours later we were marched back to our barracks. Always in formation of five rows we waited at the barracks entrance and were handed a small aluminum bowl of soup. Sometimes a few green leaves and a few potato peels appeared in the broth. Most of the time the soup was as thin as water. It had the same medicine taste that we got at Auschwitz. But any food was better than no food, and it was especially welcome after carrying those rocks.

Looking around our new surroundings, I discovered that the great majority of people here were Polish. They came from different backgrounds than we, and most probably had a different upbringing as well. I didn't know if those were the reasons, or they had reasons of their own, but they surely hated the very thought of Hungarians. It didn't take us long to learn that their hatred was deep-rooted and irrational.

We Hungarians were getting double punishment, we decided. Not only were we being dehumanized and held in prison for no other reason than the fact that we were born Jewish, and, therefore, we were hated by the Germans. Being in prison with these women was almost as great a punishment, feeling their hatred for us also because of our nationality. Our *blockowa*, Sonja, was more a beast than a human being. She seemed friendly during the couple of hours after we arrived. I asked the girls on my shelf about her. "Don't let any kindness fool you," they warned me. "Watch her tomorrow. Things change here from minute to minute."

"Why?" I asked my mother, who was laboring to speak in her limited Yiddish.

"Simply," they answered, "jealousy and envy."

"What is there to be jealous about or envious of?"

"Oh, there is plenty. You will see."

Looking at these big, oddly shaped bald skulls, skinny faces and huge uneven teeth, I wanted so desperately to talk more with them. I tried to communicate with my eyes and my hands. They chuckled at my attempts. But they managed to understand us fairly well.

Plassow was a self-sustaining camp. There were factories for dresses and shoes. They created everything right there—even their own monsters. All day long we could only hear cries of agony from men and women, and when we tried to see or listen, we invariably felt a blow to our head or back that sent us on our way.

After the first few days, numbing fear set in again. Fear completely dominated our sorry existence.

Weird smells wafted by periodically that almost choken us. Nobody could say what the smell was. The long-time inmates grew somber and silent each time the stench rose in the air. And the *capos* lessened their blows.

The lack of communication was terrible. The great majority didn't want to waste time or the effort to try to make themselves understood. Holding my nostrils together with two fingers, I tried to ask the Polish girls at the rock quarry about the smell. With tears in their eyes, they finally made me understand that prisoners were being burned.

"Burned?" we gasped. "What do you mean, burned?"

They just shook their heads. Wiping their eyes they walked on.

"Oh, God!" we exclaimed among ourselves. But why? We just didn't understand.

Going to work every morning became a routine. More and more *capos* came there, but the tall blond one who gave me the piece of bread I did not see until four days later. When I noticed him, I was thrilled. I would have liked to thank him for the slice of bread, but he was out of sight again. Then he was back, looking in our direction. As soon as he saw me, with long steps, he walked over to the spot where five of us were carrying rocks. With a smile he ran his fingers again over the top of my shaved skull. Suddenly he handed in my direction a beautiful pair of white and black shoes that looked like a perfect fit. I hesitated to reach for them, but he insisted by bending down and pushing my foot out of the canoe. Mother watched from the side, smiling with tremendous joy and happiness. The blond *capo* urged me to put on the shoes—the most beautiful shoes I had ever seen. With a big smile he took my old shoes and walked away.

I stood there dumbfounded. It was not a new pair, but they fit perfectly. My happiness knew no bounds. At night I put the shoes under my head in the straw, but on the third day my new shoes were stolen.

I cried and ran to the *blockowa*. I told her what happened. "What are you going to do about it?"

"What can I do?"

"Nothing, and I can do nothing either." She explained that theft such as I experienced was very common.

"Wait until two weeks when you go the the *entlausung* and the shower. They will hand you another pair of shoes."

"But I work!" I cried. "In the rocks!"

"So what?" she asked. "It doesn't snow there, does it?"

With that answer she gave me a shove so unexpectedly that I fell against the sleeping shelves. She didn't even notice, but just walked on in the opposite direction.

I walked back to my shelf, crying. Tears flowing, I climbed up to my shelf. Mother didn't want to believe that anybody was capable of stealing the shoes, so she spent half the night looking for them, combing through the filthy straw. The Polish girls screamed at Mother, who kept repeating, brokingly, "Me look shoe. Me look shoe."

The screams woke up the girls on the adjacent shelf, who shouted back to us, "You pigs, couldn't you wait until the morning?"

At the same time, the fourth and fifth girls on our shelf tried to pull mother's dress, but got the third girl's instead, who screamed, "Don't! It's only me!"

In the dark I wanted to change places with Mother, but she overpowered me and firmly ordered me to stay put. The girls were cursing in Polish. The Hungarians were screaming, "You animal, whoever you are!" Half the barracks woke up and called out, "Quiet, quiet, we want to sleep! Go outside and fight!" But those near us wanted to know, "Who did it?"

"Did what?" I asked.

"Shit!" one of them answered.

Mother put the palm of her hand on my mouth to quiet me down. She didn't want me to get into an argument with them. In the dark she felt safe.

"Oh, my God!" Mother said to them. "Nobody did that! I just disturbed the straw looking for my shoes."

"Why in the middle of the night? You going somewhere?" someone asked her.

"Oh, you filthy idiot!" the other one screamed.

I screamed back in the few words of Polish I had learned. Then I repeated what I said in Hungarian.

All of a sudden came the familiar sound of the whistle and the light came on. In marched the *blockowa*.

"What the hell is going on here?" she demanded.

Everybody lay motionless. Dead silence prevailed. She was going through row by row, searching for any sign of trouble, yelling, "I will beat the daylights out of you, you bastard, if I find you."

Thank God nobody said anything.

At morning coffee everybody wanted to know what the commotion was during the night. Mother pulled on my arm for me to be quiet. I volunteered, though I knew. I became the most popular person in the barracks at that moment as everybody was curious. "She was looking through the straw for my shoes," I tried to explain. "She thought maybe they weren't stolen, but got lost in the straw, and by poking and stirring it made the smell worse."

"That straw must have been there since they built the place," a woman offered, "and they have never changed it since."

The Polish women laughed and grabbed the girls next to them. Pointing to my feet they related the story to them in Polish. The girls on our shelf just stood by and smiled.

I asked everybody standing there with their coffee, "Do you

speak Yiddish or German?" When I found one who would help, I pulled her arm and asked her to take me to the *blockowa* because I wanted to ask if she would have some wooden shoes somewhere there that I could try on before I went to work.

Looking down at me the *blockowa* said, "Oh, it's you again!" She listened half-heartedly and suddenly interrupted the interpreter. "Tell her with her piercing dark eyes that she has nothing to worry about."

Mother was disappointed seeing me coming back empty-handed. But just before the whistle blew for the roll call, Mom got a bright idea. With a big smile she pulled me close.

"How could we get a pair of scissors here?"

"What do you need sicissors for?"

"To cut the bottom of your dress."

"Wait, wait, wait," I repeated, "You promised to make me a brassiere."

"That too. But first the shoes."

Before we could even discuss how to secure it on my foot, the whistle blew. We marched to the field to answer roll call.

Mom's face gleamed as if she liked problem-solving. Standing in line she asked everybody who wasn't Hungarian (because the Hungarians couldn't possibly have anything) for scissors. They looked at her and only smiled. I pulled her dress, pleading not to ask anybody any further.

At lunchtime, with her teeth, Mom opened the seam of my dress. She tore about twenty inches off, split it in half, and wrapped the fabric around my feet.

As luck would have it, we were taken to a different place to work. There we had to carry boards that men were sawing with big machines. A new barracks was to be built.

I was not familiar with that area. I stepped on everything. By evening I could barely walk. The foot wrappings fell off constantly, so I took them off and carried the dress material with me as I worked.

My foot soon filled with splinters. That evening, while standing for roll call I was in sheer agony. The agony in my mother's face spoke of her feelings of helplessnes towards me and my plight. "Please! Don't look that way! They will know that you are my mother," I whispered.

"I cannot help it. I just can't help it when you suffer like that."

I tried for mother's sake not to limp as we were marching back to our barracks, but it was impossible. The soles of my feet hurt so terribly that I winced and cried with pain. Behind me in the line a couple of Polish girls grabbed me and pulled me backward while one of them jumped into my place. Horrified, Mother tried to grab me back but the girl put her finger on my mother's mouth to be quiet and gave her a slight push to indicate that she should continue marching. Within seconds an SS woman and an SS soldier and his dog passed our side of the line. When the SS were at a safe distance the girl that had taken my place stepped back and the other pushed me forward returning me to my place. No one had realized what they had done. They had hidden me from the SS, who, if they had seen me limping, would have taken me out of the line. Mother turned to the women trying to grasp their hands, "Thank you! Thank you!" she whispered. With me at her side again, she now seized my hand.

"What do you want, Mommy?"

"I want to kiss it!" she whispered.

"Please stop it. Sisters don't kiss each other's hands."

"But this one wants to kiss it," she whispered back in my ear.

At the barracks door my mother thanked the Polish girls over and over and over. One walked away ignoring us, but the other stopped. "What's the matter with your foot," she asked me. With my eyes and hands I tried to tell her. She finally caught on and led us to her shelf. She showed us a sewing needle. Using, basically, sign language, I offered her half of my rations that night and half a slice of my bread the next day if she would lend it to me to take out my splinters. She said that she was an expert at removing splinters and for the whole slice she would do the job.

Mother agreed immediately.

Startled I said, "No, no, wait, wait. She doesn't understand. It's not her business." At once I upped my offer, promising the Polish girl my whole square of margarine with the half slice of bread, at the same time shushing mother to be quiet.

"Don't you understand," I said under my breath in Hungarian. "They don't know you are my mom, and don't act like one now. They don't allow mothers."

"Oh! I forgot!"

Showing the fingers on her hand the girl asked me how many splinters I had. I shrugged my shoulders. Now she wanted the whole slice. I said that wasn't fair. "I am hungry, too." She looked at me for a second. Then, big-heartedly, she said, "Okay. Half a slice—and all your margarine." I agreed. That was my first business transaction.

The Polish girl told me to climb up to the second level of her bunk and hang my feet over the side. I did. She grabbed my feet—almost pulling me off the shelf. The girls on the bottom shelf weren't there yet, so we had enough room.

"Well," she asked me, "where are the splinters?"

There was no water to wash away the dirt and therefore she couldn't see a thing. She spat on my foot a few times and wiped it with her arm. She still didn't see anything. So she kept spitting and wiping and spitting and wiping.

Picking with a needle, she looked up at my face for an answer. "Yes, yes! That's the place!" I responded. It hurt as she kept poking me with the needle. I yelped with each poke. When she stuck it deep I let out a wild cry.

"You want me to take it out don't you?"

Mother, wringing her hands, hopped around me. Holding me from the back she said, "Please be patient. Soon...soon...soon." Then she turned to the girl and asked her to be gentle, too.

The girl suddenly dropped my foot. With both hands on her hips she glared at mother. "What's the matter with you? You dance like a lunatic around her," the Polish girl said, imitating my mother's motions. "Be gentle, be gentle, please," the Polish girl continued, mocking mother, "you sound like her mother!"

She got back to work on my foot but then paused and moved closer to my mother with an expression on her face like she had just discovered America. She touched Mom's shoulder and asked simply, "Are you? Are you her mother?"

"Oh, no! no!" mother protested. "I am only her older sister."

The girl looked at her with unconcealed suspicion. Turning back to me she grabbed my leg, spit on my foot, and cleaning it, began poking with the needle in her quest of finding the splinters.

When she turned to operate on my second foot, the Polish girl ran out of saliva. Without hesitating she asked the women who stood near by watching her to spit on it. Wiping and digging she continued. Both of my feet hurt so much that I offered her the entire slice of bread just to let me go. "No, no, no!" she exclaimed. "We have to finish."

Thank God the girl from the bottom shelf came back and chased us away. My business associate shouted after me, "I may not have taken out all the splinters, but I can guarantee you—you have the cleanest feet in this joint!"

As much as my feet hurt, I returned to work the next day. I went to work everyday—either at the rock pile or at the building site. Each morning I hoped that I would see the *capo* again, and that he would notice that my shoes were gone. It was something to look forward to every morning, just the hope that he might pass by. One day, when I saw him walking at a distance, my heart skipped a few beats. It was easy for me to spot him because he was so tall. But it was very unlikely that he would spot me, a young girl less than five feet tall and lost in the crowd. How was I to attract his attention? I was biting my lips in helpless frustration as I came to the brink of tears.

I grabbed a pile of 2 x 2 boards and started walking. I picked up the boards too hastily that I stumbled from the weight, dropping my load with such a clatter as I fell that everybody near by rushed to help me.

The tall *capo* saw the commotion and came over. He spotted me in the center of the crowd. Pushing everybody aside, he pulled me up and took me out of the crowd.

Seeing that nothing had happened, he ordered the prisoners to return to work. I started to go, too. But instead of allowing me to return to my task, he put his big hand on my head, stopping me from moving anywhere.

With a wide grin on my face he pointed to my feet and asked me where the shoes were. I shrugged my shoulders and stretched out my arms, palms held upward, trying to tell him I didn't know.

Now laughing out loud the *capo* stopped everyone to ask if they spoke Hungarian or German. Finally a man passed who spoke Hungarian and Yiddish. For a Scandinavian that wasn't much help, but between the two of us we made the *capo* understand that somebody had stolen the shoes that he had given me.

"Oh!" he looked surprised, and stroking my face with genuine pity he repeated, "Oh! oh! oh!"

He told me to wait. Saying that he would be right back, he walked away. He turned. Pointing to the ground, he ordered me to "stay put."

Mother came by with her load of wood. I signaled to her that everything was okay. I told her that I was waiting for the tall *capo.*

"Thank God."

"Don't thank Him yet," I teased her.

Soon the *capo* returned. He carried in one hand a pair of red pumps with low thick heels. Just looking at them I thought I would die from excitement. My hand shook as he handed them to me. Then, with his other hand concealed behind his back he presented me with a package all in white.

I didn't understand what he said as he turned and walked away. I shouted after him, "Thank you! Thank you! Thank you!"

I, my mother, and those who worked with me, marveled in disbelief. The shoes were a size 5: a perfect fit. In the package, wrapped with a white triangle kerchief, were hard-boiled eggs and almost a half a loaf of bread. I couldn't believe my eyes. "Oh God! How lucky can one get?" everybody exclaimed out loud in wonderment.

Mother suddenly got between me and the people watching. "Pooh, pooh," she said. "It's nothing. It's not what it seems."

"What are you doing?" I asked her.

"I don't want them to evil eye you."

"Oh, cut it out!" I retorted. "They'll laugh at me. You want them to ridicule me?"

"I don't care," she snapped. "It's better than envy and wishing you bad luck."

It was a subject on which she would not budge. The "evil eye" was something she believed in—and feared—every bit as much as she feared the Germans.

I put on the new red shoes and used the binding from one of my feet to wrap my priceless food in. The other binding I wrapped and tied around my waist.

Standing in line for roll call, we could talk about nothing

else but our good fortune. Mom kept saying, "You see how great God is? He is taking care of us! He is on our side." She was referring to an earlier suggestion of mine that she leave God alone for awhile, since obviously He was on the other side.

After we got our soup and returned from the latrine block, I went to my business associate with a new proposition. With half a loaf of bread to bargain with, I had the chance now that I was waiting for—to buy or rent a needle so that Mom could sew me the bra that I dreamed of.

"Hey, little Hungarian, how are your feet?" the Polish girl called out. Then she saw my red shoes. Hastily she climbed down, skipping bars on the ladder, she took big strides towards me. When she got near me she pushed me back so that she could get a better view.Astonished she proped her face between the palms of her hands. "I don't believe it!" she gasped over and over. Everybody was looking in our direction, asking what had happened. In Polish she told everybody that yesterday she did surgery on my feet because I had been barefoot, and now, the next day: "This!" She gulped. "Look! I can't believe it!"

The women looked, suspiciously, for a moment. Then they turned away. Some scorned me with bitterness couple with envy.

Now assuming her famous pose, the Polish girl with the needle, put her hands on her hips. With one palm raised quickly she almost touched my face, and asked, "How did you get those shoes?"

I gestured as if I were giving her something. "Like that," I said.

"Just like that?"

I nodded, puzzled. Didn't she believe me?

Then she gestured in the Jewish way, circling her index finger around her temple, meaning "you are crazy"—the "you" meaning me. Innocently I asked her "Why?"

Annoyed the Polish girl almost put her finger through my nose. "Don't give me that innocent look!"

I had no idea what she or the others were driving at, but from that evening on I was branded. That was for sure. My good fortune had created only suspicion in others. Thank God they didn't know that I also had a huge piece of bread and an egg to go with it. If they had known that, it wouldn't have been mere suspicion that they felt toward me. "If I had known you would be so hostile, I wouldn't have come to make a deal with you," I said.

"No, no, no!" she waved her hands. "I'm ready for anything." She straightened her skirt, and asked, "What do you want? What is your deal?"

"Would you sell me the needle?"

"Now I know that you are crazy." she said with conviction.

"I'm not crazy for trying to defend myself. Why won't you sell it—if I pay a good price?"

"Because..." she was looking for the right words. She could sell the needle every day. It was the only needle in the block. She could sell it every day—a little while at a time. In other words, she could rent it—and make more than by selling it.

"Okay," I said, "for one night—how much?"

"What do you want to do with it?" she asked.

I wanted to make circles near my temple to show she was the crazy one now, but I didn't want to antagonize her too much. She asked again, and I impatiently snapped, "For sewing, you idiot!"

"The price depends on what you sew."

I figured that. I replied, "To sew a hem on my dress," and pointed to the bottom where we had torn the material off for my make-shift shoes.

"Oh, I see. What happened?"

I told her that after she had removed the splinters from my feet I tore the bottom of my dress off and wrapped it around my feet.

"And where are the rags now," she demanded to know.

"Oh, they were dirty. I threw them away."

There went the internationally known sign again, telling me how crazy I was. Naturally I didn't tell her that my mother washed the material in the latrine and was saving it to make me a bra.

I took a slice of bread from under my arm which I had wrapped in the triangle scarf. She let out a scream and reached to grab the whole thing.

"What's the matter?" everybody was asking again.

"Look! This *Wenger* (meaning Hungarian), she's got a scarf, too!"

"No! No! No!" I protested. "It's not mine! I just borrowed it to put the bread in."

"Oh. That's different." She handed me the needle and thread, and I gave her my slice of bread.

I was overjoyed, until I realized what I forgot. Mom didn't know how to sew, other than sewing on buttons. I climbed up to my shelf, feeling disgusted with my self. Mom was waiting anxiously. She gave me a big smile when I lifted my hand, showing her the prized needle and thread.

"Wait! Don't be so happy," I said. "Remember? We don't know how to sew!"

"Don't worry. We'll figure it out."

We stretched the two strips of material, both full of stains and holes from being used as shoes. "I can sew these up, don't worry. It won't be anything difficult," Mom said. "Easy job. Don't worry."

"How are we going to cut it?" I asked.

She thought for a moment. "Now *that's* a problem."

It was the first time I heard the word "problem" from her.

She bent over the ragged shreds of cloth and went to work. She flattened, twisted, turned, pulled, and finally claimed, "I've got it!"

Tearing it bit by bit in every direction that the material allowed, mom produced what may not have looked like a brassiere, but it was a brassiere to me—the most cherished one that I ever owned. She made a hem on my dress, too, to give my dress a finished look. She also made a belt out of the narrow string that I had used the day before to tie the rags to my feet. My happiness was complete.

The next morning, at 5:30, I was the first to climb down the shelf for coffee and the roll call. I had kept my shoes and hers between mom and myself all during the night. They were safe there, and they were easy to find in the dark.

With my bra on, the belt around my waist and the white kerchief on my bald head, I felt like a human being again.

While I was standing in line for the coffee there were cries, "Look at her! Where did she get that?" pointing to my head. "Or that?" others protested, pointing to my belt.

"This? I got this from the bottom of my dress," I partially explained. I was the center of attention. Everybody was asking me questions or exclaiming over my unexpected fortune. Thank God, except for the three Polish girls on our shelf, nobody knew about my bra.

When my turn came for the coffee, the *blockowa* dropped the laddle back into the coffee and pulled at the kerchief on my head. Fortunately I had tied it securely. She demanded to know where I got it. She looked me up and down, and spotted my new red shoes. Roughly she pulled me out of line, motioning to her helper to continue serving coffee to the other prisoners.

She exclaimed, "Aha! aha! aha!" pointing to my shoes. "Where did you get those?"

"From a *capo*."

"What kind? With a yellow star?"

"No, a triangle."

She looked at me suspiciously.

"Ask her!" I said, pointing to my mother. The *blockowa* did not even know that we knew each other. "She saw it," I insisted. I pleaded with the *blockowa* to ask her, in fact to ask all the girls in my *Kommando*.

The *blockowa* blew her whistle bringing everyone in the barracks to attention. "Who was in her *Kommando* yesterday?" she grilled. "Who worked with her? Come forward!" Nobody came forward. "I am not going to hurt you!" the *blockowa* screamed. "I'm just asking a question! Come forward!"

Some girls eased forward to see who I was, but I was so short that they couldn't see me—not even if they wanted to.

Finally a few came forward. The *blockowa* asked each one exactly what they saw, and if they had seen with their own eyes the *capo* give the scarf and the shoes to me. Each said "Yes." Finally, convinced, she gave me my coffee and shoved me through the door.

I asked one of the Polish girls standing next to me at roll call why I had to prove who gave me the shoes. "Because you didn't have them the day before, and she thought you stole them," she responded.

"That bitch!" I swore. "She didn't care when I complained that mine were stolen! Does this mean I have to report to her any time I get something?"

She shrugged her shoulders. She didn't know. She never got anything.

"How long have you been here?" I asked.

"One and a half years." She spoke listlessly, without caring, without hope.

"Oh, my God!" I whispered.

From the roll call formation, three rows, three rows of prisoners, including Mom, me, and thirteen others, were marched toward the main exit of the Plassow camp.

"Oh, God! Oh, God!" we all gasped as they ordered us to stop. We had no idea what lay ahead.

Two SS men came out of a building and over to us. They pointed to the gate. "March!" they ordered. As we moved they handed us over to two other German officers who were not SS.

We walked out of the camp, but not to freedom. We only got a smell of it.

We marched for about an hour to a deserted area. We feared that they would shoot us for sure. Our knees trembled. Mother grabbed my arm, whispering, "Don't get scared. Just don't get scared. God is with us. You know that."

"Oh, they will shoot us for sure," many were whispering.

"Don't be silly," Mother whispered back, trying to calm everyone. "Why would they bring only 15 of us? They could have gotten a few more. There are plenty back there!"

The two soldiers came back from what looked like some kind of a crater, a large cavity in the ground, the kind of place that Polish girls had described where people were shot and buried. But instead of shooting us the soldiers handed us some pails and showed us where to fill them with water. Then, after making a washing motion with their hands, they motioned us to follow them. They took us to the crater and inside it, all around were anti-aircraft cannons, and in the center was a low, squat temporary structure where many soldiers lived.

We were handed shirts and underwear to wash. Some, like Mom, were put to work sewing socks and buttons on to clothing. We were amazed, and even more startled when the soldiers gave us some bread and a small piece of sausage at lunchtime. We took a bite or two and put the rest aside, saving it to take back to our barracks. When the soldiers saw what we were doing they smiled and made motions with their hands that we should it right then and there.

We had almost forgotten what meat tasted like. We kept

marveling at our good fortune while we washed the soldier's clothes, and wondered how we could wash our own. "Don't worry," one of the Polish girls said, "This week we all will get a bath and new clothes, because once a month there is *entlausung.*"

It was about time for us to go. Such good news in one day! We hoped it would never end!

We stopped working much earlier than in the camp, and were told that we would be called back tomorrow. We jumped up and down with joy. The soldiers laughed, and handed each of us a slice of bread.

Marching back to the camp we were passed by Polish peasants. They stared at us for a while—spoke with the German soldiers, and a few seconds later they reached into their bags and handed me and a few other girls two or three bunches of green onions.

I was afraid to take the onions at first. But I took them anyway. Suddenly I felt that the whole world was mine—not because of the feast I could have with the fabulous extra food, but because it would give me something of value to trade. The girls seemed happy for my good fortune, even those who didn't get any. "At least somebody got something," they said.

I waited to see what my mother would say. It would either be "Thank God," or "Pooh, pooh," to protect me from the evil eye.

Walking back took about an hour. We were handed over to the SS at the gate. I was too scared to move, fearing that the onions would fall out from under both of my arms. I looked back at mother who was carrying the third one under her arm. She gave me a reassuring feeling as I slowly passed the inspection. We were told we didn't have to stand for the roll call, but could go directly to our barracks.

After being discharged we headed straight to our barracks and didn't stop until we were safe on our shelves. The other girls were still at roll call, so there were only a few of us there. Mom and I hugged and kissed each other, thanking God over and over again for our good fortune.

After we got our soup, when the rest of the group came back from the roll call, I told mom that I would take one onion and sell it for bread. Then, if I could, tomorrow I would sell another one. Her eyes were shining at the thought alone. Full of hope, she wished me good luck as I climbed down the ladder.

She watched me each time I climbed down, always saying, "Watch your step. Slowly. Slowly."

I looked back from the bottom of the step and said to her, "I could use a little praying now," and with my bunch of onions I left.

Everybody wanted to know where I got them. "They are for sale," I replied.

I headed for the bakery, stopped for a moment in front of the building, and, hoping it was the right place to stop, stood outside, showing people what I had. They all turned around and in a few seconds had circled around me, asking how much I wanted for the onions. I didn't understand what they were saying, so they asked on their fingers. They pulled out some *zlotys*, the Polish currency, each worth about ten to the dollar.

"No, no, no," I said, "no money. I want bread, only bread."

They motioned excitedly for me to wait and not deal with anybody else.

In a few minutes the bakery worker was back. He asked again, "How much?" I pointed to the loaf of bread under his arm. He handed it to me, took my bunch of green onions, split it into two bunches and at once traded one of the bunches to another bakery worker—for a whole loaf of bread! He had come out of the deal with more than he put into it. I watched this transaction and said to myself, "Maybe I have learned something."

I took the scarf from my head, wrapped the round loaf of bread in it and, trying to get their attention, said, "Tomorrow I will bring more onions." They finally understood what I was saying, and shook their heads happily. They responded, "Okay. We will be waiting here for you tomorrow."

I turned and ran all the way to mother. She was waiting anxiously at the barracks door. I lifted my package high, running breathlessly towards her.

We couldn't believe our luck. We broke off a piece of the bread and ate it while walking to our shelf. We kept the rest of it covered with my kercheif so that the others wouldn't see it.

As we basked in our riches it dawned on me what would happen during the night. Oh God! They may steal it! "No!"

mother said. "Only three girls here know."

"And that is plenty," I said. "What do you think happened to my shoes? It wasn't someone from the outside who stole them." I thought for a moment, and then said, "You know what? I'll go back and find out how much money the bread costs, and I'll sell the onions for that amount. Then I can buy bread, a half a loaf at a time. It will be much easier to guard."

"That's a good idea," mom agreed. She stayed on the shelf, guarding our bread, while I wrapped two bunches of onions in my kerchief and went back and stood near the bakery. I offered the onions to those who passed by, and after I found out how much a loaf of bread cost, I sold both bunches—each for the price of a loaf of bread. The money I put in my shoes and ran.

When my mother heard me climbing up the shelves, she looked over at me, searching for answers in my eyes. I shouted excitedly, "Yippee!"

"Thank God!"

From the excitement we could barely sleep. The Polish girls watched us and realized that there must be something good going on. They asked, "What's the good news? What are you so happy about?" They got no answer from either of us.

I suggested to mom, "Let's eat up our bread! Let's have one good meal!" We ate half of the loaf, pinching out a little piece at a time. "This is the last bite! No more!" we'd say. "Don't take any more!"

"Oh...just one little bit more" and we'd break down and nibble another small piece.

Mother wanted to leave the rest for the morning, but I was afraid that during the night it would be stolen. "No! no!" mom assured me. "I will hold it in my hand."

"How?"

"Like this." She tied our kerchief around the bread and squeezed it—and me—close to her chest.

Before the morning came, before the whistle blew, I woke up and found my mother sobbing. "Oh, my God! what's the matter?"

"They stole it! They stole it! They stole the kercheif with the bread!"

One of the girls on our shelf woke up. "Be quiet! Be quiet!

You're going to wake up the people. Quiet down!"

I begged mom, "Please, don't cry. We have some *zlotys*, and tomorrow I will trade them for some more bread when we come back from work. Don't worry! We're going to that paradise—outside the camp. Just think of that!"

As we kissed one another over and over, we whispered to each other not to worry. We talked of the two good days in front of us. "We are going to that wonderful place to work again," and "afterwards I will buy another piece of bread!"

We were fortunate. Our *Kommando* was called out again, and we marched to our heaven on earth. We had the same task as we had performed the day before, and we were treated, again to a slice of bread, handed to us by the soldiers, as we stepped into the crater. As we grabbed for the bread they watched us. Amused, legs spread, arms folded, they took in the comical sight, trading jokes over the eagerness with which we ate.

We washed and cleaned their living quarters. Late that afternoon we marched back to the barracks along the same path. The same Polish peasants came by, bringing two more friends with them. This time they were carrying a whole bag filled with bunches of little red radishes. They gave each of us two bunches. Surprisingly the Germans allowed them to do this and permitted us to accept the radishes.

Some of the girls ate theirs right there. "What is sure is sure," they said. "This way nobody can steal them from us."

Back in prison I ran to sell one of my bunches as soon as I was allowed to leave the barracks.

After a month at Plassow, we were marched to the *Entlausung*, as the Polish girls had predicted. I went barefoot, leaving my red shoes buried in the straw on our shelf. I didn't want to take a chance on losing this pair. I also left my bra and belt with my kerchief, for they were treasures impossible to replace.

Again we exchanged clothes. I got a long-sleeved gray wool dress. Two of me could have easily fitted into it. The opening of its V-neck reached down to my belly. The hem almost dragged the ground. It was too late to go back and try for another dress, and the pair of shoes that they gave me, again of mismatched sizes, looked to me like men's shoes.

Once we received our clothes we were marched forward to

be sprayed with the de-lousing powder, then we were ordered out and back to the barracks.

"Don't despair," mother comforted me. "Everything works out for the best."

Back at the barracks I ran to rent the needle. It wasn't available. The Polish woman put me on the waiting list.

I told her that I had a pair of men's shoes and she could have them if I could get the needle right away. "Where did you get the men's shoes?" she interrogated me. I told her."Look! the Hungarian again," she called out to her friends, tapping on her temple. This time, however, she was calling me clever instead of crazy.

"You lied, in other words!" she declared.

"Just a bit!" I answered, showing her the end of my little finger. "Just a little bit, because they really stole my original shoes, you know. You certainly know about it because you took the splinters out of my foot."

She understood me and agreed. "Okay," she said. "It's a deal."

I was glad to get rid of those men's shoes—although I had hoped to sell them for bread.

Punishment was severe for lying and stealing, yet to survive deception was a necessary evil. When she mentioned lying out loud, it frightened me because it attracted the attention of the others. One more scare like that and I would have given the shoes to her for nothing.

The Polish woman saw the fear come back and knew that I wasn't so smart after all. Once she saw that I was "just as Hungarian"—meaning "dumb and vulnerable"—as I ever was, her tone dropped, as did her respect for me.

There were no mirrors anywhere, so we didn't know what we looked like, except from the laughs of the girls around us. In order to make me look as decent as possible, mother tore off the bottom of the long wool dress, hemmed it with the rented needle and rolled up the sleeves. I still had the belt that she had made from the other prison dress. Only the neck remained a problem.

If somebody had given me a good shake the dress would have fallen off my shoulders through the scooped neckline.

We didn't know what to do. We asked the girls on our shelf. They replied, sarcastically, "Why not turn the dress around and let the opening be at the back." In the front, at least, there was something to hold up the dress.

I solved the problem by taking the material mom was going to make me a panty with and used it instead as a scarf around my neck. The scarf hid the gaping opening. It also gave me a terrible rash and caused me to itch constantly. Most of the night I scratched myself. Mother did the same, probably from working with the wool. In time, fortunately, we both got used to it.

I decided on one solution to the itching at night. "You know what?" I asked mom. "I've been naked almost all day anyway. I'm going to take this off and sleep naked." But when I slipped under the cover the straw grated on my bare skin. I moaned, "Ouch!" throughout the uncomfortable night until mom pleaded that I put the dress back on. I didn't know which was more unbearable: to be scraped by the straw or to itch from the wool. I scratched all night, to the point that I was almost bleeding by morning. Mom had done the same—but quietly.

Since I could not sleep that night I puzzled over who had taken our place at the gunnery position outside the camp while we were sent to the *Entlausung*. We had gone straight to the barracks, and from the barracks back to the *Rockommando*— the working detail on the rock pile. It looked as if our good luck was running out.

Standing in line for coffee the next morning, mother did the strangest thing: she constantly touched my neck on one side and then on the other. She had an odd expression on her face.

"What's the matter with you?" I pulled away from her constant picking.

"Nothing, nothing. I just saw some flies. That's why you were itching."

"Oh." I moved on.

During roll call, the SS soldier walking with an SS woman halted the count as they reached our row.

"Hey you, *Negus!* come here!" he ordered.

We couldn't tell who he was yelling at. Nobody moved.

Again, pointing at our row, he called, "You! you, *Negus!*" Now he got closer and pointed directly at me. "Come here!"

My palms began to sweat. My mouth was dry. My knees, I felt, would buckle from shaking. My heart thumped.

I walked forward. He grabbed my shoulder, and holding it firmly, asked something that I did not understand, except for his last question, "Where are you from?"

"Hungary," I whispered in German.

He asked if I spoke German. I shook my head "no."

"Any Hungarian speaking German, come forward!" he shouted. Nobody moved. "You all that dumb?" he asked with a wholehearted belly-laugh.

Now a few came forward. He kept one as an interpreter. He sent the other back.

He asked where I got so black. *Negus* means "black" in German.

"At the *Rock-Kommanda*," I said.

"Would you like to work in the kitchen?"

I just stared at him, almost straight up. My eyes barely came up to his stomach. I had lost over 20 pounds by this time. I had not had a complete meal since I left home in March. I couldn't remember what it felt like to work in the kitchen. Vigorously I nodded my head "yes!"

"Tell the *blockowa* that tomorrow you will have to report to the kitchen, and you will have to leave before the roll call." With that he shoved me back into the line. Still sweating, but relieved, I took my place in front of mom. She was breathless from fear. We reached for each other's hands as I got in line. I gave her hand a quick squeeze. I half turned and managed to give her a smile. I saw the muscles on her face relax.

They called our *Kommando* to work after the roll call, back to the soldiers' place outside the camp. As we moved forward so did another bunch of girls—the ones who had replaced us while we were at the *Entlausung* the day before. We all pleaded to go. To shut us up the guards let both groups of 15 go.

As if he knew it was my last day there, one of the soldiers gave me an extra slice of bread. Another sneaked over and gave me a piece of sausage. I thanked him over and over. He just ran his fingers through the one-and-one-half-month-old black fuzz on the top of my head, smiled, and walked away.

When the Polish peasants met us on the way back this time, the same fellow who was there two days before took one look and his chin dropped. He must have thought, correctly, that he was seeing double, because we were two *Kommandos* now. He was not prepared for so many people, but he offered us what onions he had. Everybody reached for them, but only the few got small bunches—and again I got one!

There was joy among the lucky ones. There was saddness and bitterness among the unlucky. Threats and curses became vile. These outbreaks of furious envy frightened me, but I resigned myself to hearing them.

Mother decided that this was a treasure that we would not sell. It would be our feast alone.

We compromised. I sold half of the onions. We promptly ate the other half.

In front of the barracks was the only place we could act as mother and daughter and talk alone. I asked, "Mommy, why are our fellow prisoners so mean? Why are they so rude and so vicious?"

"Oh, my darling, don't look at it that way."

I couldn't believe my ears. "Mom! Are you pretending!"

"No, no! I am only hoping and believing."

"In what?"

"They are mean to us only because they are hungrier than we are."

"We are in the same boat, aren't we?"

"Yes, but a few times we got something extra. Like now. That means an awful lot. And it makes a great difference, my darling. They are still very hungry, and, for us, it will be a little bit easier again tomorrow."

Climbing up to our shelf I found our straw to be a complete mess. "Surprise! surprise!" I exploded as mother climbed up behind me on the ladder.

Frightened, she asked, "What happened?"

"They were looking for something again!" I stared at them: our three shelf mates. "You did this!" I accused them. "What were you looking for?"

"Yeah!" one snapped back. "We were looking for your brain!"

I had other problems. Barely had I sat down when I began to itch again. Mother tried to get my attention away from my discomforture, but the itching got worse. As I grabbed hold of something by my fingers to see what it was that was biting me, mom hit my hand and caused it to fall. "What did you do that for?" I asked. But before she could answer I grabbed my neck again. At the same time the three girls next to me laughed out hysterically. The could not understand what we said to each other, but from her actions they saw that my mother was trying to spare me the discovery that we were totally infested with lice.

"Oh, my God!" I said. "They must have put them there." I was ready to fight the girls.

Mother grabbed my arm. "They didn't put them there. They were here already."

"When did they come?" I asked, horror stricken.

"Who knows?"

"What do you think you were scratching all night long from?" my Polish neighbors asked, rolling with laughter. They were imitating my shock by holding their faces in their hands and whispering, "Oh, oh, oh," sarcastically.

We just had a bath. Now we have lice!

"How is that possible?" I asked aloud.

"You were not aware of it before?" one of the girls asked.

"No," I responded. "Maybe I didn't pay attention."

"Didn't pay attention? Didn't you see it?"

"No," I answered. "I wasn't aware of lice crawling on my body." Then, hurt, I puzzled, "How can you be so indifferent?"

They just looked at me. "There is nothing we can do about it."

I asked the girls on the other shelf about the lice. "You did not know?" came their startled inquiry. "Are you crazy? They were here before we were!"

I went to see the *blockowa* to talk to her about the kitchen. She was busy talking. I stood there, waiting. After a half an hour she saw that I was still standing there. She asked what I wanted. I told her that I was to report to the kitchen.

I was scared of her. She had always asked questions of me to which I didn't know the answers. Mother had urged me not to be scared. "Just tell her simply that you are to work in the kitchen," she instructed, "because she will have to account for you at the roll call."

"Where? Where are you going to work?" the *blockowa* demanded to know.

I called the interpreter. "In the kitchen," I responded.

She wanted to know, in detail, how I was picked among the thousands of women. I told her exactly what happened.

She shook her head in disbelief. She called out her repertoire of Polish insults, and finished with, "What luck for a Hungarian! Only the luck of a Hungarian!"

The next morning I headed for the kitchen. I had to walk the entire length of the camp to get there. I discovered all kinds of places that were new to me, and I started in every direction wondering what they were.

At the kitchen the girls already were working. They scorned me, "We don't need you. Go away!"

"But the SS officer told me to come."

A girl who looked like us but acted like a *capo* went into what looked like a large glass cage where the huge SS officer who had picked me was sitting at a desk. He looked up. She pointed in my direction. He strode out, yelling, "Oh, you, *Negus!*" He ordered the girls to put me to work washing the tubs in which coffee or soup was carried to the prisoners.

My hours were longer than those who worked in other *Kommandos*, but it was a tremendous advantage working in the kitchen. Not only could I eat an extra bowl of soup, or even a potato, when no one was looking, but I could steal and take back to the barracks extra food for mom. Stealing was very dangerous. If caught, prisoners "disappeared." I was lucky. I was never caught.

Before I even opened my mouth the kitchen prisoners, indiividually and collectively, despised me. As I scrubbed a tub, one of them came up behind me and shoved me hard, causing me to fall into the tub. As I cried out, they gathered around the tub, laughing hysterically. I climbed out, crying, but continued to scrub diligently.

In the evening, before I was told to go back to the barracks, the SS officer gave me an aluminum bowl with a cover and a little handle. He said I could take it with me, but to bring the bowl back tomorrow. The bowl was filled with soup. So happy was I with that bowl of soup that I forgot, or at least pretended to forget, what the girls had done to me earlier in the day.

Mother and I drank the soup, eating the potatoe peelings

we fished out of the broth with out fingers, eating them as if they were the most exotic and rare delicacy. We thanked God for our good fortune.

The three girls next to me wanted to know how I got that full bowl of soup. I was laboring to explain to them that I worked for it, but they stopped me abruptly. "I bet you do!" one said insultingly.

Mother snapped back at the girl's implication. She knew what they were thinking. At the moment I didn't understand the insinuation.

"We work, too," they said in chorus. They picked off a few lice from each other and threw them toward us. "You see? This is what we get for our work!" They picked off additional lice from their clothing and threw the creatures in front of us where they landed on the straw. Turning, the girls crawled into their spaces, laughing crudely to themselves.

Huddled together they spoke Yiddish. I only understood a word here and there. Mom angrily showered them with words. They only urged her to "go away." Words meant nothing.

Frustrated, mom turned to me. "Don't pay any attention to them," she instructed.

The girls in the kitchen made my second day another total hell. When, in the evening, the huge SS officer showed up, he screamed, "Hey, *Negus*, come here!"

The girls watched anxiously to see what was in store for me. From behind his back he handed me a colorful dress. This was "the brute," as they called him. His name was Hans Kundi. He was from Hamburg, I found out later. He carried a whip and was known and feared for the way he lashed out with it constantly in every direction at anybody near him. Now he handed me a dress that seemed to me to be the most gorgeous thing in the world. While the girls working in the kitchen watched wide-eyed from a distance, the SS motioned for me to go back in the rear of the kitchen and put it on — "*Los! los! los!*"

The dress had a black background design on which were printed very bright yellow, white, pink and deep red roses surrounded by green leaves. The material was of European cashmere, like fine linen, with short bouffant sleeves that looked like two balloons. The slim torso descended to a tiny waist and a full skirt.

I tried with my saliva to smooth down my two-month-old fuzz so that it would show under the front of my kerchief. It wasn't long enough.

As I walked back the girls snapped sardonically, "There goes the prima donna!"

The SS officer smiled and said, encouragingly, "Good! good!" He turned and walked away.

The *capo* said something to the other girls. I did not understand her. She shoved a tray in to my hand and told me that I would be serving him his food from now on in his glass cage (a room about 12 x 12 that was situated so that he could see in every direction and thereby was in total control of the kitchen).

I took his tray into him. It had been prepared by the Germans, not by the prisoners. He motioned for me to wait once I had placed the tray on his desk.

He was built like a tank. His face was huge like his frame. He had a sense of power about him. The whip, from which no one within his reach was safe, dangled from his hand.

I froze before him. He reached out from where he sat and put his fingers on top of my head. This was a simple act for him as I was only about 4 feet 11 inches. He was over 6 feet tall. He laughed. His belly shook while he tried to tell me not to be scared. He saw that I was petrified.

The officer gave me a piece of meat. I held it in my hand while he watched. Silently he motioned to me that I was to eat. Pointing again, he commanded, "Eat!" I did.

He asked how old I was. He wanted to know, also, how long I had been at the barracks. I pointed to his desk at paper and pencil. He handed them to me. In Goatish letters I began to write. First he looked at me. Then he drew closer and looked at what I was writing. "You can write German?" he asked with great surprise. "You can write Goatish? And you cannot speak German?"

I told him that I could only write. I learned how to read and write German. I didnot learn how to speak German.

"*Negus!*" he exuded, "that's wonderful, it's *wunderbar!*" I could see the girls watching intently from outside the glass-walled office.

He gave me another piece of meat. He motioned, again, for me to eat.

"This is for my sister, my sister," I pleaded, pointing in the direction of the barracks.

"Oh!" he said, and calling out to the *capo*, he instructed her to bring a *menaska*, a small aluminum container with a cover, like the one he gave me the day before. Into it he spooned the leftovers from his plate.

He couldn't understand, nor did I, how I could read and write perfect Goatish and not speak a word of German. He kept shaking his head. I just shrugged my shoulders and turned out the palms of my hands, showing that I did not know either. He laughed even louder than before, shoving his tray on to my open palms. Turning me around he pushed me out of the door.

Since the *capo* had served the SS before, her only ambition now was to destroy me. She was waiting for me as I left the glass cage. Jumping me, she dragged me toward the rest of the girls who were all waiting behind the biggest boiler. It was the only place in the kitchen that was hidden from the view of the SS officer. Arms on her hips, legs apart, her face almost shoved into mine, the *capo* barked, "What happened in there? What did he say? He gave you his food, huh? And what's for us?"

"I don't know what you are talking about!"

"What did you do there?"

"Nothing!"

"You liar! You bitch!" She slapped me across the face. "I saw you writing!"

"I only showed him that I could only write but not speak German."

"Did he ask you to write?"

"No."

Another slap was administered to the other side of my face. "Who told you to write? You volunteered? You whore!"

What is a whore, I wondered. What's she talking about?

"He gave you the food. What did he give you the food for?"

She was interrogating me roughly. I didn't know how to answer. She slapped me again, over and over, left and right. I raised one hand, and pointing with the other to the aluminum bowl, I explained, "He just gave this to me for my sister."

"You hear that, girls? This lucky whore is even luckier than we thought. She has a sister, too!" and she slapped me again. "This goes with this," she screamed, pushing her finger almost into the *menaska*. "This goes with this to your sister!"

I was helpless and powerless behind the big boiler where the SS couldn't see. If he could, he probably wouldn't have bothered to help me.

I could have killed her right there. And she could have killed me. The difference was that she had the power to actually do so. I didn't.

The girls dispersed, leaving me there, cursing the *capo* to myself. I sank down sobbing, swearing that I would have revenge someday. I picked up my old dress, covered the *menaska* with it, and ran to my barracks.

The *blockowa* was talking with some of the girls at the entrance. They stopped as I drew closer. She looked at me as if I were from outer space. She grabbed one of the bouffant sleeves as I was passing by. She pulled me back, roughly.

"No so fast, not so fast, Hungarian! What's your name?"

"Ebi," I said.

"What kind of a name is that?"

"Hungarian."

And before the word was out of my mouth she slapped my face. The two girls watching held their bellies laughing. The *blockowa* put her index finger under my nose.

"So you are a wise one, huh?"

"I only answered your question. You asked 'what kind of a name is that', so I said 'it's Hungarian'."

"If you're so good with answers, let's hear more. Where did you get that dress?" She began pulling both my beautiful bouffant sleeves up in the air.

"From the SS."

"Oh! So you are a whore!"

"No! No!" I cried. "I work there. In the kitchen. Remember? Yesterday I told you!"

"And he gave you this dress, today? And that, too?" she asked, pointing to the *menaska*. She pulled off its cover and jammed all five fingers of one hand into the food, and then licked them. "Hmm! Good!"

The second the *blockowa's* attention was diverted, I tore myself away and ran to my shelf and climbed up to my mother who was resting on the straw. She didn't reach out to great me as usual. Seeing her lying there frightened me. She sat up, and with a faint smile said, "Hi!"

"Look what I brought you!" I exclaimed as I handed her the container of food.

"Oh! how beautiful you look!" she sat up and hugged me. "Oh! how beautiful!" She turned her head over her shoulder, and spoke her famous "Pooh, pooh, pooh," against the evil eye. "What a beautiful dress! Who gave it to you?"

I told her.

"Oh, thank God!" she whispered.

With every bite, with every sip of the soup, she insisted that I eat, too. I told her I had plenty.

While mom ate and marveled at how pretty I looked in that magnificent dress, I saw that she was not her usual self. I suggested that we go for a walk.

For the first time, she said "No!"

"Oh, my God," I worried. "Mom," I whispered in her ear, "what happened? What happened today?" This was the end of my second day in the kitchen. It was the second day that I had not worked with her. It was the longest we had been separated.

Mom said it was nothing. I insisted that she tell me. She responded that her leg hurt. Looking at it I could see that it was red and swollen.

"Don't go to work tomorrow. I will talk to the *blockowa*."

Mom stopped me. "Don't go down," she said. She would know more about how she felt by morning.

"No, no, Mom," I said. Climbing down I went to the *blockowa*. I told her that my sister's leg was red and swollen and that she was not herself. She said, "All right. I will report it. Tell your sister to stay up on the shelf."

I did not tell mom about the *capo* in the kitchen, or the initiation I had at my new job, because I knew that that would upset her. She went on all evening how grateful I must be to God and how she was doubly grateful to Him for being so good to me.

I dreaded the morning and going to work. How scared I was of the morning. How much I had looked forward to it before this morning had come. How scared I was today.

Walking in to the kitchen early the next morning, I said "good morning," and nobody responded. Anything that I touched the *capo* grabbed out of my hand. "That's not your job."

"Then what is my job?"

"To take your ass and get the hell out of here!"

I found some trash to take out, so that I could be out of her sight. At the disposal area, behind the building, I saw the SS officer. This huge brute seemed like a different being from the one who had laughed at me and had given me the dress and the scraps from his plate. He was beating to death a poor soul who was picking something out of the garbage. Like a raving maniac the SS was shouting and beating and kicking the ragged skeleton who lay motionless in his own blood.

The man was either dead already or bleeding to death as the German turned and walked back to the kitchen. As I re-entered the building, the SS was busy beating someone else—a Czechoslovakian girl who worked there. He shouted and swore at her, lashing her with his whip. As he saw me walk in, he stopped. His manner changed. Suddenly transformed, with his smile of yesterday in place, he called out, "Hey, *Negus*, how are you? Come here, *Negus!*"

I almost dropped. Every time he saw the fright of terror in my eyes and on my face, he laughed louder.

"Come here!" He spoke with an urgency in his voice that I couldn't ignore. He grabbed a head of cabbage from a big box and thrust it into my hand. Then he turned me around and kicked me in the behind. Roaring again with laughter he walked away.

He not only looked the brute, but God, he was one. He was a man with a thousand faces and moods that could change from murder to merriment and back again in a split second. He must have been insane.

When I returned that evening, mother was not there. I asked everybody, but nobody had seen her. I went from shelf to shelf.

Finally the *blockowa* "remembered." The cruelty of that woman was unmeasurable. It was she who had removed my mother. She would have known, anyway, because it was the *blockowa's* job to account for every single barracks' inmate. My mother was in the infirmary barracks.

I ran all the way to the back of the camp. There I was stopped by another *blockowa* who wouldn't let me in. I pleaded and begged, but she pushed me away each time I went near the entrance of the infirmary.

I couldn't tell her it was my mother. "It's my sister," I said.

"A sister," she pronounced, "can wait until her sister comes out."

"But you know that nobody comes out from here alive!" I cried bitterly. "Please, just for a minute. Please, let me see her!"

Annoyed with me, she stung both of my cheeks with two sharp slaps and ordered me to go away at once. I didn't dare stay there any longer. It was getting late. I hurried back to our barracks.

Lying on my lice-infested shelf, scratching myself raw, I cried out loud at my loss and my fate. The girls on my shelf softened somewhat when they saw me cry hour after hour. "Don't worry," they said. "Don't cry. She will be out soon."

But now, with one space empty, they had more room for themselves, and thus, they had a little more comfort. From exhaustion I fell into a sleep that entered oblivion.

The next day at work I scrubbed the outside of those huge tanks, tears falling freely. I couldn't stop them.

Each day I went to the hospital barracks with a little soup for my mother. I sent it in with the *blockowa*, because she wouldn't let me take it in myself. Each day I sat on the ground in front of the hospital, crying, begging the *blockowa* to let me in for just a second.

I looked for someone else with authority to let me in, but everybody I asked kicked me or pushed me or cursed me in Polish. There was not one blessed Hungarian with any authority there or anywhere that I could appeal to.

My mind wandered and became prey to disturbing desires. Oh, I wanted so desperately to kill that grotesque bitch, that hospital *blockowa*. But I just didn't know how.

She would grab the soup each day, and in a few minutes she was back with the empty *menaska*. Once as I stretched, hoping to get a glimpse of my mother, the *blockowa* gave me a shove and I fell against a pole and from there to the ground. All I could do was to silently curse her.

Finally, one day as I sat on the ground outside the infirmary, I began sobbing desperately, crying out loud, "Mommy, mommy! I am here, mommy! I am here!"

I didn't care who heard it. People stared. Some stopped and

and asked, "What's the matter?" I am sure most thought I was crazy.

Selections went on daily at the infirmary. The SS went through daily, pointing who would live another day, and who would be taken away in those big trucks, never to be seen again. Some were already dead as they were dragged naked by one arm or one leg from the infirmary building—another one of the horrors I witnessed and which turned into memories that follow me like shadows through life.

A week of sheer hell passed. I was seeing the same scene repeated daily. I prayed. I prayed that mom would not fall victim to their systematic murder. But I was losing hope.

For me tomorrow was something I no longer looked forward to. I practically no longer cared. In desperation I decided to try something reckless.

After work and roll call I went to the bakery area, bought a part of a loaf of bread with the rest of the money from the sale of onions and put the bread in my bouffant sleeve. I approached the infirmary *blockowa*, handed her the soup and placed her hand on my sleeve, telling her what it was. I offered her the soup and all of the bread. She hesitated. That gave me hope. Then, with a single motion, she pulled the bread out, reached for the *menaska,* and shoved me in—pointing in the direction where my mother was.

At the sight of her I almost fainted. She lay there nude. A dirty rag was all that half-way covered her body.

Mom was dozing. She awoke and looked at me dazed. I fell into her listless, weak arms. She mustered all the strength that she could to hug me, showering me with thin kisses from those parched lips.

I pulled an entire potato out of my bra. The joy her face registered when she took her first bite is now and forever engraved on my heart and soul.

"The soup was part payment for letting me in. I gave her all of the bread to let me in to see you."

Mom shook her head. "What a shame. You shouldn't have done that. You should have eaten it."

Under the glare of naked bulbs, hundreds of suffering, equally naked women lay waiting for death. The eyes bulged out of the skulls of many of the near-cadavers who pitifully begged for food and water.

"I'll get you out of here, I swear!" I ran to the *capo*. "Please let me take her out!"

Looking at me with suspicion the *capo* said, "You have gone completely mad!"

I grabbed her arm, trying to stop her from walking away from me. She shook my hand off. I caught her's again. "How much?" I whispered.

With no hesitation she replied, "Thousand *zloty*," and left me standing there.

This was definitely no hospital. There were no doctors. Nor was there any medicine. Besides the horrible stink and smell of human waste, there was an air of uncertainty, an atmosphere that drew a thin line between life and death.

It was a scary place. A deadly place. Gray, gloomy and gortesquely sinister, the hospital was more of a morgue than a center for healing. The occupants were not treated as patients but as numbers. They got only coffee and soup at night—no water, no bread. The only thing that kept my mother alive, she told me later, was her enormous love for me.

On the way out I whispered to the *capo*, "Don't let her be taken out. Please. I'll bring the money tomorrow. Please don't let them take her away."

I only had 500 *zloty*. What was I to do? I couldn't sell the extra dress. Now mother would need it. Her dress had been taken away.

At last I had the answer! I could sell my shoes, my kerchief and my belt. This I did easily—and quickly, and with their sale I had the price of my mother's freedom.

I raced to the infirmary the next night and found the *capo* at the door. I told her that I had the money she required, and handed her the old dress to take to mom. In minutes they were at the door. The *capo* took the money and said to us, "Keep walking," and shoved mother next to me. "Keep walking. Don't look back. Keep walking!"

It was one of the happiest and proudest moments of my life rescuing my mother from the barracks of death. She was so thin that the wind could have carried her off. I found out that the soup I took to her each day never reached her. The *capo* ate it.

Mom's concern immediately turned to me. She didn't think

of herself. "Where are your shoes?" she asked.

"They stole them," I lied.

'Oh, my God! Oh, my God!" mom exclaimed.

"Don't worry. Next week we're going to *Entlausung* and I will get another pair."

I asked the *blockowa* what I could do to work with my sister again.

"Are you crazy? You want to give up working in the kitchen?"

"Yes. Please help me. She just came back from the hospital. I would like to stay with her and work with her."

The *blockowa* shrugged and said I should go to the kitchen before roll call and tell the *capo* there that I wanted to be assigned to a different *kommando*. "You won't be working there any more, and then in the roll call in the morning, wherever they take her, you go with her. It's as simple as that." It was "as simple as that" because "wherever they take her" was, as the *blockowa* knew, back to the rock pile.

Going back to the rock pile was terrible. We had lost much of our former strength and could barely lift those heavy rocks. As we stooped to our almost impossible task, we saw more of those living skeletons on the other side of the rock pile. Four or five of them were hastening their own death with each step they took. They dropped their load and fell on the rocks, crying out in pain. The SS grabbed one man by the arm, another by the leg and pulled them like pieces of string, flinging them off to the side. Others, still on their feet, walked aimlessly or indifferently. They were detached from any kind of feeling, looking no longer capable of hatred or revenge. All were unmistakably on the very brink of death.

Mother always urged me not to look at these scenes. "When you are ever on the boundries that divide life from death," she said, "you need not bear witness. Please. Please, don't look. Please, don't look any more."

By now our extra portions were depleted. All my money had gone to the infirmary *capo*. There was nothing left to sell, and we were terribly hungry.

I decided after roll call that I would go back to the kitchen. Maybe the SS brute would see me and give me something.

"What happened to you?" He was looking at my bare feet, black fuzz on top of my head, no scarf and no shoes.

"I don't know," I shrugged in the way that made him laugh before. He laughed, again, from his belly. "Please," I implored, "let me work in this kitchen after the rock *kommando.*"

The *capo* standing beside the brute told the SS that they didn't need any more help. "We have more than enough help." Her eyes blazed at me. "We don't need her."

The SS ignored her. "How about some soup? You want soup? You want to carry it to your barracks?"

He instructed the *capo* to give me some soup to drink at that moment, and to let me have some more to take with me. He gave the *capo* a push and told her to find a *menaska,* and when she pretended that she didn't hear, he ordered, "Give me yours."

I became desperately afraid. Now the *capo* will kill me for sure, I thought. The SS noticed my panic and with a belly laugh he pulled me to the glass cage. He emptied some scraps from his plate into the aluminum container, added from his tray and filled the container with soup from one of the boilers. When he was done he gave me a push in the back and told me to come back the next day.

Once I had returned to our shelf, the girls beside us noticed the unusual container of soup. With disgust they taunted, "Your business is flourishing again, huh?"

I had no idea what they were talking about. I had a hard time understanding Yiddish. Not only were the ordinary words difficult, but the insinuations were next to impossible.

From my mother's reaction to their words I began to understand what they were implying. To make certain that I did understand them they shouted, in Yiddish, across to the other shelves, "Tell her! Tell her!"

Obscene words were shouted as the girls on our shelf rolled with laughter.

"Don't pay any attention to them. Don't listen to them!"

"How can you ignore that?" I asked mom.

"You must. They are jealous, and they envy you."

When I came back the next day from the kitchen with an oversized pair of high-topped laced shoes on my feet, my reputation was sealed. Not only in my barracks, but, as I found out later, my reputation was sealed throughout the camp.

Mother and I formed a shell around ourselves as a defense. It was forced upon us, and after the daily abuse from those girls the shell almost closed.

Coming back from the latrine, two Polish girls next to me asked me where I got the fancy shoes. Fancy they were not. They were ugly, but the lacing kept the shoes securely on my feet.

I didn't want the Polish girls to know that I got the shoes from the SS in the kitchen. That would have brought on another flurry of crass comments. I told them, therefore, that it was none of their business. Responding to my comment one of the girls tripped me. I fell. Sprawled on the ground I grabbed her feet, causing her to fall a few feet from me. Mother rushed to help me. The Polish girl's friend helped her up. After straightening her clothes, she showered me with a bath of Polish curses. Once she had vented her anger she walked away.

"They call Hungarian girls not only stupid, but blind and mad," I lamented. "I told them that I was none of those things, regardless of what they thought." I told her that I fought back just then because I knew it was then or never. Since I was much younger than they, and had more strength, "I had to show them," I told mom. "I'm not afraid of them."

Summoning all my courage, I continued. "Don't you see? Here only the strong survive. I won't...I can't let them bully me any more."

"Please don't pay any attention to them," mom pleaded.

"Mom?" I asked. "Don't you understand what I mean?"

"No," she answered. "But if you tell me, I will."

"Do you really expect me to let someone trip me, fall on my face, and not pay attention to it or to them?"

"Let's not talk about it," she said after a moment.

By the end of August 1944, we were about 50,000 prisoners at Plassow. Not one able-bodied man or woman was left in that god-forsaken place. Mother and I were as bony and hollow-eyed as any of them. The first and last to come there were now indistinguishable. Everyone was ground down together by the SS, the *capos*, and the life of slave labor.

No longer horrified at the thought, we now lifted lice off of each other as an absent-minded pasttime. The great majority of men and women showed no concern, no hope, and gave no effort to do anything much except to forage for food, instinctively resisting death.

One evening, holding my little container of soup, hiding a whole raw potato for mom in it, just before making my last turn to head for the barracks, a hideous, very near-shriek startled me from my usual listlessness. Nothing that I had heard at Auschwitz was more terrifying.

I turned in the direction of the scream. Two living skeletons motioned for me to go away.

Peeking on tiptoe through a small crowd I saw two SS soldiers restrain a prisoner. The victim's screams intensified as one of the SS held and kicked him while the other slid a rope around his neck. Prisoners near by stared into space. I grabbed my mouth with both hands, stiffling a cry, and stood there unable to move.

The SS dragged their victim a few feet by the rope tied around his neck. They hoisted him up so that he hung from a pole that was held in place by some other prisoners.

Two prisoners next to me grabbed my arm, making me drop the bowl of soup to the ground. The top came off. The potato rolled out. One of the two picked it up and bit into it savagely, like the starving retch he was. The other man grabbed him and snapped, "Give me a bite!" They both fell to the ground, groping and growling like caged, wounded animals.

I picked up the container and tried to walk. I couldn't make my legs move from loss of strength brought on by a fear that was more intense than I had known before. Now there was dead silence. I didn't hear the shrieks anymore. Yet I still couldn't summon the courage or energy to move.

In my frozen state I looked at the scene before me and my view was unimpeded. The Germans had gone. A dreadful looking skeleton was struggling to pull the broken shoes off the hanged prisoner's feet. The two prisoners who took my potato ran to the pole, grabbed the man attempting to remove the shoes, and shouted, "You dirty bastard! Don't you have any heart left?"

The one pulling on the shoes cried bitterly, "But he gave

them to me. He gave them to me!" and raised his hand over his head to protect himself from their blows.

Neither of the other prisoners listened. The two crazed ones kept kicking and cursing the third. The weeping man let the hand protecting his face drop. "Please," he implored, "please, listen to me—for a minute. Don't hit me, please." He was kneeling on the ground, sobbing. "He gave them to me," he repeated. "He told me that I could have them." Then, pointing to the hanged man, he said, "He was my brother!"

I wanted to cry out. I couldn't. But at last I managed to move.

Horror stricken, holding my mouth with both hands, I ran toward my barracks, screaming continuously. Girls along the way tried to stop me to ask what had happened. I tore myself away from them. I ran and ran as fast as I could, running to find my mother.

The door of the barracks the *blockowa* stopped me. She asked me what had happened. I tried over and over to explain it to her, but I couldn't. I just couldn't.

A couple of girls from the bottom level of my shelf grabbed my hands and pulled me in with them, trying to find out what had happened. I was hysterical, and repeated over and over, "that was his brother...that was his brother...that was his brother...." More girls collected around me. Others from the top shelf peered down.

"What happened?"

"What's wrong?"

One of the girls slapped me, trying to bring me to my senses while she demanded, "Stop it! Quiet down!"

Through the shrieks and cries my mother recognized my voice and climbed down. Seeing me lying there and the girl slapping me, she screamed, "Please! please! don't hit her. Don't touch her!"

"Nobody is hitting her to hurt her," the girl replied. "We just want to stop her from hurting herself."

They pulled me, still screaming, up to a sitting position.

"Talk to her, you idiot! Talk to her!" someone said to mom who was close to fainting. "Don't you see how scared she is?"

They ordered me to look at my mom. Slowly I began to calm down. Mother was kissing me and stroking my fuzzy head with one hand, and squeezing my hand with her other, whispering softly, "My darling, my darling," while trying to totally cover me with her own body, kissing me, and crying over me.

Some of the girls solmenly, and softly, remarked to one another, "Oh, my God! What a sister she has!"

Mother raised her head. Turning towards the girls, she spoke softly. "Thank you girls. Thank you very much!"

Suddenly, unexpectedly, the girl who had slapped me, slumped down and kissed my mother's hand. Then she kissed my mother's face.

The other girls stared at their companion, looking at her as if she had gone crazy. When the girl stood up, straightened her dress, she remarked, "Don't stare, you idiots. Can't you see. She is her mother! She's got to be. Don't you see how terribly concerned she is? Don't you see how she is kissing her, and holding her?"

The girls looked at us. They were silent.

We said nothing. We just climbed up to our shelf. Once there, Mom turned to them and promised, "I will pray to God to help you, and to repay you, because I surely can't."

Bending up close to mom, the girl who slapped me asked her, "Are you? Are you?"

Mom motioned with her eyes. They said "yes."

I asked mom why she admitted it. She stroked my face. "Don't be afraid. From them we don't have to be afraid any more." Then she asked what happened. Why did I fall apart? What upset me so much? Did anybody hurt me? She inspected me from head to toe, looking for wounds.

"No, Mom, no."

Mom had the fantastic ability to ignore what she didn't want to see, but I didn't. I saw what I had that day very clearly, then and now. The helplessness intensified the feeling of anger, and I swore revenge.

I didn't tell mom of the barbarianism I had witnessed. I knew that she didn't have the strength to bear it.

The next day, marching to work, I saw the big black and gray trucks up close. They were loaded with motionless human forms that were barely alive. They were practically on top of each other. We had to stop to let the trucks pass.

"The last luxury," one Polish girl said scornfully.
"What does that mean?" I asked.
"You don't know what that means?"
"No."
"What do you think?"
"Is this like Auschwitz? Is this the same?"
Silence.
"The trucks have the same big canvases as at Auschwitz..."
She looked at me hard. I froze inside. I looked again at the helpless prisoners.

The girl reached over. Closing my mouth, she gave me a push and said, "Come on, dummy, go!"

Each day we returned to the rock pile to discover that by some evil magic the rocks got bigger overnight. Mother asked, "Why don't we think of something else? This is really our imagination. This is only in our minds."

One of the women that mom was talking to said that she had a terrible belly-ache, and that she had to relieve herself at once. There was no toilet, so she squatted next to a rock. The SS and their dogs were there in seconds, and the same horrible shrieks of terror that I had heard the night before came from that woman's direction. Let off their leashes, the dogs became the woman's executioners.

"Don't look, don't look, don't look," mom kept repeating as she reached for my head and pulled me in her direction. "Just keep working, please."

An SS called two girls who were standing closest to him, and ordered them, *los, los, los*, to carry away the mutilated body. As they pulled the bloody remains of the poor woman across the ground, one of her legs held to her body by only a narrow strip of flesh dropped off. The dogs pounced on it. In frenzy they devoured it.

We worked for a while, quiet, speechless, in the darkest despair over any hope of survival. All we could hope for was for the day to end. Seeing what we could not avoid seeing, we could find no humanity left in many around us and none in any of the SS. "Show us God. Blink so we'll know you're here," I whispered. Drained physically and emotionally, I retreated into oblivion.

Cruelty was increasing with the SS. We didn't know why.

We were running out of ways to co-exist with it. We could disassociate ourselves with the evil that we were powerless to fight, mother suggested. But turning our heads away from one evil only meant that we would be confronted with yet another in the SS catalog of horrors. Wherever we looked the SS were there. They were at every end of the camp. They were at the gravel pit, where periodically prisoners were lined up, told to strip, and then shot and shoved in. Some prisoners were killed for specific reasons. The majority of those executed were but of a liquidation plan of the Germans who were determined to bring about "the final solution": like a "bug-spraying" of an entire race of people.

Every time I witnessed the condemned line up at the pit, I would close my ears within my hands and hide behind the soup boiler in the kitchen. Many times while I was walking to work at the kitchen at five o'clock in the morning I would see tortured yet living skeletons pull dead skeletons by the arms or legs and throw them like rags on top of each other; then, with ghostly sweeps, pour gasoline over the cadavers and ignite them, burning the dead Jews like so much trash.

Nobody could take survival for granted—except for the triangle *capos*, or, at least most of them. They seldom spoke with us. They had no interest in us. In nearly every case I knew they were treated different than the Jews, for they were not Jews. They knew that they could and would go home after the war. With this "assurance," they didn't live in constant fear of dying. They gained their superior status and attitude because of this and because when they were punished, they were not punished— as severely as were the Jews.

The cruelest triangle *capos*, along with the German SS, were those from Germany and Poland. These *capos*, like the Germans took out their frustrations on the most convenient target: the Jews. These *capos* were like the Hungarian Arrow-Cross. These *capos*, like the SS, used and abused their power like it was their hobby. They were ruthless and barbaric animals. Their actions made me wonder if they had souls. Interestingly, these *capos* adopted the same mentality as the rest of the prisoners. They envied their neighbor's portion to the same extent that we did. Yet they had the power—the power to kill—to obtain that which they lusted for: bread, a potato, soup, or anything else.

Mother, with her customary tolerance, had an explanation for everything. The non-Jewish *capos*, she theorized, had similar backgrounds: like the Hungarian Arrow-Cross. From childhood they had heard their parents blame the Jews for everything. Since the majority did not understand our language, they kept to themselves, not asking us, visiting with us or communicating in any way. They were not necessarily snubbing us; their ignorance of us made them avoid and hate us.

"But why?"

"There is no point in asking. It really makes no difference, now. And, since we have enough problems without them, why bother to even think about them? Just stay out of their way."

I was walking outside the barracks with mother during this conversation. It was the only place we could have a mother-daughter relationship. On the shelf we only slept, hoped, and prayed together.

Mother was concerned about me getting into a fight. She didn't want me to get involved in any kind of barracks brawl, no matter what happened. "With these desperate people," she said, "it is very dangerous."

"But to fight or confront them," I argued, "sharpens my senses." I paused to look at her. "Mom," I continued, "they steal anything and everything. I cry because what they steal is mine, and there is nothing else that I can do."

Puzzled, I asked, "Why do they steal? Why do they steal, no matter how little it is?"

"Because they are hungary."

"Oh, come on. So am I. So are you."

Softly she replied, "You must reserve your strength, and, please, apply some self-discipline."

"But Tibi always fought back. They were afraid of him."

"I know."

"And so I gave it back to those Polish girls before, And I will do it again. Getting a few extra necessities has given me a reputation, but then I'm sure this will also get around: that from me they can expect to get back whatever they give. I can't fight back against the *capos*—or against the *blockowas*, but I can fight against the rest, Mom, I swear that I will."

Chapter Eight

Back to Auschwitz—September 1944

There was no need to fight in Plassow anymore. The next morning, after the roll call, we were marched to a fenced-in area that was prepared for the women during the night. We panicked. Nobody knew why we were there. It was late September, and toward evening it got chilly. We sat on the ground, waiting, but didn't know for what.

The only light we had was the light sweeping the grounds from the high tower. It was not late, but it was dark. In the noise of so many people, I heard the shout, "*Negus! Negus!*" The SS from the kitchen was there at the barbed wire with a little package in his hand. He handed it to me, telling me not to be afraid. "They won't kill you, but you are going back to Auschwitz. Don't tell anybody." He wished me good luck, and then left.

All the girls had stepped back, afraid of him, when the huge SS came near. Therefore, they couldn't hear what he said to me. Though showing disgust, and envy, on their faces, they were dying to know. Mother pulled me away from them, fearing that their accusations would provoke me to fight.

In a few minutes the SS was back. "*Negus! Negus!*" he called out louder than before. He came to the wire again, and asked me, "*Negus*, would you like to get out of here?"

"Me? Get out?" I stammered. "How?"

"I take you." He showed me his hand. "I take you out."

"Oh, no thank you," I recoiled, "I won't leave without my sister."

"Okay," he said. "I take your sister, too."

"We would get killed," I enjoined, "but thank you."

"I am going to Hamburg," he came back, "I will take you with me."

"I am too scared. But thank you, very much."

He reached for my hand. "God be with you," he whispered. He turned. He left.

"What was that all about?" the girls interogated me as they reassembled around me. Mother pulled on my arm, cautioning me not to say anything.

We slept on the ground, a couple of thousand of us. At daybreak, columns five abreast, we were marched to the railroad again. Once more we were shoved in, 80 women to a boxcar. I had told a few girls where we were going. By morning everybody knew, and we all knew that it wouldn't be a long trip. We resigned ourselves to our fate, sitting in the boxcars, now without any straw on the floor. It was not so much the hard floor, nor the bumps we had to endure which hurst us so much, instead it was the absence of a toilet that caused us the greatest discomfort and anguish.

At Auschwitz we had to face the most dreaded fear of all: the nefarious selections of Dr. Mengele. We whispered instructions to each other: "Walk erect. Smile."

With a flict of his thumb Mengele motioned mother and me in the same direction where the majority was: the direction of the living. "Thank God!" mom whispered. I countered, "Don't say 'Thank God', yet!"

In columns of five we were marched over to the Birkenau camp, near the crematoria. There, without any straw on the shelves (but the same three-high layers of boards), the women were jammed like corded wood. And, as occured with each new arrival, choas broke out and prevailed.

A semblance of quiet was restored by the *blockowa*. The *blockowa* was a real beast. She had the eyes of a demon: eyes that burned with such hatred and fury that we obeyed her by sight command.

Once on our shelves we talked. We talked about the bodies we saw piled up on top of each other as we passed the railroad station. We talked of little else. We talked of the carnage, eventhough we had seen so much, for it remained a horrifying sight.

Mother and I got a lower-level shelf. We considered ourselves lucky. The barracks was a madhouse of women who had just been through selection. Girls, now separated from sisters, or who waited and screamed in anguish waiting to learn what had happened to a relative, filled the shelves. Like playing cards we were being shuffled back and forth, loads of us, one after another, coming from all over the growing German empire.

Girls, with bulging eyes, shouted from my shelf. They appeared so horribly disfigured that I couldn't bear to look at them. The whistle blew, and the cries became only moans that didn't seem to stop.

We were told we were in Birkenau Lage B, which didn't seem much to us at the time. After nightfall, they announced a latrine call. Afterward, we lay like herrings next to each other all hungry yet everyone too exhausted to care.

After roll call the next morning we marched again, quite a distance. We were consumed with a fear of what might be in store for us. This fear gnawed at us incessantly.

As we marched we noticed, coming toward us, one of those skeletons in a striped uniform pulling a cart full of rags. As he got closer I let out a scream and grabbed mother. "Oh, God!" I exploded. "Look! Look! That's my brother!"

"Barna! Barna!" I shouted. He stopped. He searched the crowd with his eyes. I was waving madly with my arms while the *capos* on the other side of the ranks searched for where the noise came from.

Barna saw me. He waved back, screaming, "Where's mother?"

"Here!" I motioned, pushing mom forward where she could see him.

"Where's Dad?" she called.

"He's in the barracks!" he shouted back.

"How are you?"

"Fine," he responded. "Just fine."

We told him, "The same! We're all right!"

He was waving with both of his hands, throwing kisses at us. We did the same.

A *capo* discovered us, and showered me with those stinging slaps to the face. Oh, how I wished to turn and give it back, to hit her back. But the joy of seeing my brother was worth every blow.

We got our shower and shave, and we were handed gray prison dresses and pairs of wooden shoes. We were then sprayed and herded into another room. What now? we wondered.

We saw a group of Polish girls standing behind a long table. Mother turned my head. "Don't look!" she commanded.

"Oh, my God!"

"Don't look, my darling. Don't be afraid. Don't get scared. It's nothing. It won't hurt," she whispered.

I saw the girls ahead of me. I cried. They were being branded like animals. They were writing numbers on our arms with needles and blue stains. "But here," I pointed to my dress, "we already have a number." One of the women behind the table grabbed my arm like it was a chicken about to get its throat cut. She shoved mom's arm under her arms to hold it still and began tattooing: A17503, she wrote on the skin, and then pushed her forward and grabbed my arm. I cried at the needle's first jab. The woman must have felt sorry for me, because she stopped for a second and said, "I make it small if you stop crying."

They not only broke our backs and spirits, but they put their mark on us as well. Shaven, sprayed, and now tattooed, we marched demoralized back to our barracks. Why was this necessary, we puzzled. Now we have two numbers: one on our dress and one on our arm.

There were high electric wires between each section (or Lage), in Birkenau. In Lage A on one side of us we saw men. In Lage C, on our left, were only women. The women stood by the wire some distance back. We called out to one another, asking the same question: "Where are you from?"

Everybody was looking for lost loved ones. People were being thrown together from all parts' of Europe. Chance meetings were rare. The one benefit for us was that more Hungarians were pouring in, giving us an opportunity to talk to our people. After a week went by we learned that Lage C contained many Hungarian women. Spotting them, we called out, asking for their cities and towns to see if they were near our relatives. It is difficult to express the screams of joy that erupted when some discovered a friend or relative—sometimes even a sister! The capos didn't stop us from calling across the electric wires. They warned us only, "Don't get too close." Frequently, when one woman in a section spotted a sister in the next, the two became so excited that they instinctively ran toward each other—and got glued to the wires. In terror the other women just stood there, screaming as their sisters or other relatives were electrocuted. It became an everyday sight seeing girls lying there along the wire. Some, we found out soon enough, did it on purpose. Death promised a peace life could not give.

Mother didn't want to look for anybody any more when she saw the girls falling off the wires. She told me, constantly, "I don't want to know. Let them be well, but I don't want to go to look."

Lying on our shelves one evening, a girl said that she found a sister in the C Lage from the same town as my grandmother. Mom got terribly excited. She could hardly wait until the morning. She rushed to the fence, pushing me away. Cautiously she advanced to the wire, shouting the name of the town. Across the fence an emaciated creature in long prison garb called back, "Margit! Margit!"

I grabbed my mom as she reached forward, almost touching the fence. I shouted across to the other one as she reached to touch mom, "Stop! Stop! Don't come closer!" She finally heard. She stopped.

It was mom's sister. She had recognized mom's voice when mom called out.

It was a deliriously exciting moment. The joy of seeing my aunt, and hearing that her sister and two cousins were with her there made it the happiest day in that camp.

They had an extra pair of panties that they brought with them from some other camp that had not been taken away from them—because they had not been to *Entlausung* yet. They wrapped the panties in a rock and threw it over the fence to me. They were shaped like tennis shorts and were twice too big for me to wear. But God! was I lucky! This was my first underwear since our arrival from Hungary. Or so I thought—until I saw them. The panties were dirty and full of lice. Mom offered, "Don't you worry. I will kill the lice."

"I won't wear them. Let's sell it for a ration of bread."

Mother was insistent. By the evening she said, "Look! Check for yourself! Not one louse left."

She tied the huge panties around my skinny little frame. It covered me, almost to my neck, like I was still a baby. Like a mother would think, "it looks fine," she pronounced, after she finished pulling and tucking. "There," she concluded, "Now you've got it!"

At the morning whistle, and the lights went on, I found mom awake. She was sobbing silently.

"What's the matter?" I was afraid again.

"Somebody stole my bread."

She had hidden a slice of bread under her arm. It had been a piece from yesterday's ration to give to me in the morning, to put it in my mouth, as she customarily did. During the night, she lamented, she had turned over, and, she concluded, somebody stole it.

We could barely move on the shelf. Within days the lice overtook us. On our shelf we agreed that each night we would take turns, one person per night, removing our dresses while we slept. In this way, one at a time, we would get some relief from the constant wearing of the lice-infested clothes and at the same time we would not be touching each other's bodies.

We discovered that if we all slept facing the same direction, we had more space than otherwise. So we called out, "About face!" everytime we wanted to turn to another lying position. If anyone did not want to move, the rule was that she had to reverse her position, lengthwise, and lie with her head next to everyone else's feet.

One night, all of a sudden, the last girl in our row jumped up, screaming, "You dirty bastards up there!" Someone on the shelf above had urinated and the urine had fallen on her. The girl had wanted to move, but there was no place for her to go. Discontented, she laid there, cursing.

Someone from a neighboring shelf called out, "Consider yourself lucky! Imagine if it was diarrhea!" We all laughed.

A week after our arrival at Birkenau, the *blockowa* came and blew her whistle for attention. "Today we begin *Blockspare*." she announced.

We still had many things to learn.

They lined us up next to our shelves. Two SS women followed by SS guards marched along each row, pointing at those who looked weak or especially skeletal, and motioned to the *blockowa* to separate them from the others. When the separations were complete, those singled out were marched outside. We never saw them again. This new selection process was done every day in our barracks, and as we learned later, in all other barracks.

From our shelf two women were taken. One of those taken turned to mom and whispered, "Please, take care of my Erzsike."

"They must be mother and daughter, too," mom confided. The girl, who was my age, cried all night. We tried to console her, saying her friend would be back soon. We never saw "her friend" again.

Some days later they took part of C Lage to Bergen-Belsen. After we came back we attempted to find mom's sisters again. They were gone.

Toward the end of the second week, my legs were swollen and red. One leg got so swollen that I couldn't stand on it. It was *blockspare* day. I was chosen immediately and sent to the Birkenau infirmary.

The SS stuck me on a shelf, handling me like some kind of a package. Attendants carried people in and out all day. I heard constant moans for "water," "water," "water".

In the evening I heard mom's voice, calling, "Ebi! Ebi!" She was hitting the walls of the infirmary barracks.

"Here! Here!" I answered.

"How are you, my darling?" she whispered through a crack between the wooden boards. She pushed through a potato peel and a tiny piece of cabbage leaf that got mashed in the squeeze through the wall.

"Just swallow it," she ordered.

"Where did you get it?"

"I passed by the kitchen and found it in the garbage."

How could she? I wondered. There was no way that she could have gotten near there. Nobody from the barracks could go there. I was confident that she had stolen it from somebody.

On my third day at the infirmary the *blockowa* rushed by my shelf and said, "Smile! Always smile!"

A few minutes later a gaggle of SS officers came in. Among them was Dr. Mengele. He stopped by each shelf, looked in, and pointed with his finger to the *blockowa*. She made a note with the clipboard. Then they moved on to the next shelf. Finally they came to my shelf. I had never seen the men who accompanied Mengele before. They could have been doctors. I didn't know. They stood in stone silence while Mengele spoke. He looked at me. He asked, "How are you?"

I smiled as wide as my lips would stretch. "Fine!" I exuded. "Thank you!" I spoke loud and clear. He smiled back. They moved on.

I didn't know the danger I was in until the *blockowa* came

back late that evening. Mengele was making selections in the infirmary, she said, "He will be back."

She brought me a culotte, a type of a skirt, and a gray prison dress. "Can you put this on?" she asked in a whisper.

"I don't know," I whispered back.

"You must! You must! You are too young!" she pleaded. "Try, come on! Try!"

She helped me to step into the split skirt. I just put the dress over my head.

"You need...you must...you must..." she continued. "You need this under...so you will look heavier...."

She tucked the clothes around me and pulled me by the hand toward the door. She pushed me outside. She waited there with me, watching attentively everything that passed. A large group of columns of five people passed by, coming from the latrine. "This is your barracks," she noted as a column came near. "Go back to your block. Go back! Good luck to you! Do not give up!" she whispered, kissing me on the cheek, and thrusting me in among the marchers.

I marched back terrified. I was thrilled to see the barracks. I saw it as my freedom from the infirmary.

Sneaking up to my shelf, I hugged and kissed my sleeping mother in the dark. I couldn't see her face, nor could she see mine, but I whispered, "Don't get scared, Mom. It's me!" Although we couldn't see we touched each other's wet faces. She whispered, "Thank God! Oh, my, thank God!"

At last I was grateful for my too-long dress, for my long dress covered my red, swollen legs when we were roused and marched in the early hours of the morning, after I had just got back from the infirmary, to yet another selection. Once again, Mengele flicked his thumb to the left for mother and me.

Five hundred, exactly half of the group that we were in, were sent to the right. We never saw them again. The rest of us were herded into boxcars, again 80 to a car, for another journey to a place unknown.

Chapter Nine

Augsburg–September 1944

There was no straw on the boxcar floor, but before the SS bolted the door we were each handed a slice of bread and a small square of margarine. We all began to pray, each in our own way, for none of us knew what this trip meant. We feared for our lives. This could have easily been our last meal.

"Why don't we think of better things," religious girls suggested. "Why don't we all pray to God?"

Mother couldn't thank God enough for saving me, and for sending me back to her in time.

"Mom," I noted, "the *blockowa* is the one you should be grateful to. She's the one you should thank."

"Oh, my darling, as long as I shall live I will thank both of them: God and her." She squeezed my hand to the point that it almost hurt.

We spent two days and nights on the train, moving forward and then backward. We arrived at a station that looked like it had been bombed. We had no idea where we were until we were mached amongst buildings that looked more like a private enterprise rather than a prison camp. We were taken over by differen soldiers and by SS women, but we were not pushed as they marched us to a building that had been converted for sleeping.

Walking into the building we couldn't believe our eyes. In a large room were two layers of bunk beds, each separated from the others, with a straw mat, and an individual blanket on every one, plus a pillow for each of us. A wash basin and a shower were in the next room. Then they showed us the English toilet. "Oh, God!" we were shouting, jumping for joy, "Hallelujah!"

"Pinch me!" everyone said. "Then I'll know this is real!"

The Germans stood there, watching our excitement. They were smiling. They seemed surprised—and concerned about us. We were a pitiful sight to see: bald, emaciated, in sagging, tattered prison clothing.

They waited patiently for our noise to die down. They did not scream for us to "shut up!" They called for those who spoke German to step forward. A few who stepped forward were selected as official interpreters. My inadequacy in the language frustrated me at that moment. I promised myself I would make every effort to learn it, if ever I was given a chance again.

A tall interpreter spoke to us. She was attractive, despite her bald head and prison uniform. She had a human, strong air about her that the Nazis had not destroyed. She was soft-spoken and like no one I had met in any of the camps or shelves before. She told us we were in Augsburg, Germany, at the K.U.K.A. Ammunition Factory, where we would be working. There was nothing to be afraid of. They would not harm us—as long as we did as we were told.

Later the SS selected women from among us to work in the kitchen. As promising as that selection was, it was not our biggest surprise.

At Augsburg we got real coffee in the morning, and a slice of bread with a small square of margarine. The next day we also received a small square of marmalade. It was the first sweet thing we had tasted since our ordeal began. After work we got soup and another slice of bread. The food was more than we had dreamed of.

Mother got a bottom bunk. I got the top. Marta, the interpreter, the tall girl that I admired, was in the row next to me. This led to a close friendship between us. She was about my brother Tibi's age—maybe 19. She was definitely the most wonderful person I met in the entire length of my captivity.

It quickly became October, and with the changing of the month it became increasingly chilly. The roll call was every morning and every evening, but we didn't have to go outside. It was done in the room, and we didn't have to stand for hours waiting for it to be completed.

The next morning, at 5:30, the *blockowa* (in this case an SS woman) made us realize we had not gone to heaven—not just yet. She came with a group of German civilians and some SS and supervised the picking of about 20 girls—including my mother and me—to stand aside. After the selection was completed we were marched to a railroad station where members of the German public were waiting for trains. They gaped at us, pulling back as if we were lepers. When it came time to board, they refued to enter the same car with us.

We traveled about 30 or 45 minutes before arriving at a forested area where, hidden among the trees, was a huge factory building. Inside were two rows of giant machines lined up on both sides of a narrow walkway. We were each assigned a machine and German civilians were there to instruct us how to operate them.

I was put behind a machine that was almost as tall as I. A little steel cabinet stood next to it. A civilian German was trying to explain in rapid German how to operate it.

"Wait! I don't understand!" I told him. I called for Marta, who was with us but was busy interpreting for the others who also needed help with German.

We were confused at first, but the Germans told us to take it a step at a time, "first get familiar with the equipment," which was used to make airplane parts and ammunition. Soon we were learning, quickly.

Across the aisle from us French prisoners operated the machines, but upon our arrival stopped to stare at us. They couldn't figure out where we came from or who we were. Their expressions were of curiosity and of pity as well. We could see that they had not been as badly treated as us, but that, like us, they were not permitted to speak to one another at any time. The SS guard made sure of that as he paced up and down in the center divider. He had a harsh, angular face, and he was always scowling. We wondered if he ever got tired of holding his face like that.

There were night and day shifts, and within a week everything got organized. I worked nights one week, and days the next. The male SS took us back to our barracks at night. The female SS, called Fanny, took us to work in the daytime. She was a very pleasant-acting woman, in her middle twenties, tall and slim with long blonde hair turned under at the bottom. She had a long face to match her long arms and long legs. She was very kind, but we were on guard against change at any time. We simply did not trust anyone in the SS.

On the night shift I saw mom only rarely—when I met her going to work as I was returning. But on Sunday there was no work and we spent a wonderful day together, at the end of which we got the most fantastic soup for supper—full of potatoes and ground beef. It was the best meal we had had so far; it remains in my memory as the best soup I ever ate.

Even during the week, when the ingredients were fewer, the soup was like a banquet compared to Auschwitz soup. Our two slices of bread a day, with margarine or marmalade, were also an enormous improvement.

We were issued a dress and a pair of panties a few days after our arrival. Our joy and excitement leaped some more. Conditions had improved, and we were daring to dream aloud—that eventually we might be freed. The SS room warden kept the dream from becoming too extravagant. We were instructed, in a state of perpetual rage, that she was not a *blockowa*, she was a *frau auseherin* (or woman supervisor). She walked from bunk to bunk between us and gave a kick of her boot to anyone who was in her way. She was the only cruel individual that we encountered there.

The *frau auseherin* had high cheekbones and heavy jaws. As a stereotypical member of Hitler's "chosen race," she had blue eyes and blonde hair—although it was a dark blonde. Her hair flew in all directions—even when no wind crept up behind it. Whether she was angry with us or not, she always spoke to us standing with her legs apart, hands on her hips. We quickly learned to avoid her when she was aroused as her hobby was kicking defenseless women.

There were three sisters on the beds facing mine. They were dark-complexioned, dark-eyed girls, who like me, sported black fuzz for hair. Gizi, the oldest girl, was not necessarily the wisest. Ella, the next oldest, was the most calm. Ari, the youngest, seemed to be the most sensible, and she was the prettiest of the three. Then I discovered that there was a fourth. She was named Borka. All were taller than I—but then so were most people.

On Sundays we sat on our beds and talked about our work. Working in the factory was an experience for all of us. We each worked on different airplane parts—or on different stages in the making of ammunition.

We talked about extra pieces of bread that some passing worker might squeeze into our hand. Those who overheard this, and weren't so lucky as to receive the extra bread, made sarcastic suggestions and comments that started arguments and bred contempt. Mother and Marta instructed me never to mention things that could cause envy.

After a week of the luxury of riding the train, we were made to walk to and from work at a place called Lowald. It was a distance of ten to twelve miles. People stared at us as we walked through the town each day. If they wondered who we were, the big yellow star we wore should have told them what they wanted to know. They had seen the yellow star shortly after Hitler's ascent and his pogrom against the Jews began. These were the same citizens who said, after the war was over, that they had never heard of a concentration camp.

The town's youth spat on us and shouted obscene curses. Some of them threw gravel at us. Others looked at us with disgust. But the majority of the people just walked by, pretending that they didn't see us. Of course there were always a few, a slim minority, who handed us whatever they could spare. That is where and how I got my first piece of sausage since working for the soldiers at Plassow. Oh, what a treasure it was! One girl claimed that the man who handed it to me meant it for her and she tried to grab it out of my hand. I almost fell, ducking her blows, blows which attracted the notice of an SS. The girl ran back to her place in line. I slipped the sausage into my bra to take to mom. The SS saw no commotion and left.

When the SS had gone, people around me asked what had happened to the sausage. "Did you eat it?"

I shook my head yes.

Marta was behind me and had watched the whole thing. She stepped forward, patted my head, and stepped back. That reassuring pat from her gave me a sense of security that I needed. All the way to work I was showered with sarcastic remarks.

During the night shift the guard at the factory occasionally took a nap while sitting at his post in the narrow aisle separating the two rows of machines. It was during those times that the Frenchmen watched us and passed near us, talking in French. But with the exception of Marta, nobody understood what they were saying.

After about two weeks of working there, one of the prisoners came into my part of the factory to visit his friend who was stationed at the machine directly facing mine. His name was Lucian. He was shorter than his friend. He wore a turtleneck sweater, and had a round face, dark curly hair, and big dancing eyes. A pipe hung negligently in the corner of his mouth.

Lucien began motioning to me first with one hand, then with both. I had no idea what he wanted me to understand. After a while he gave up. He tried again. I still didn't understand what he wanted.

I had to go to the latrine, and went to the SS to ask permission. Lucien took that opportunity to run ahead of me, then, walking backwards in front of me, to the other room, he tried to draw my attention to the top of a dividing wall. He pointed at the top of the wall. There a little package was placed. He motioned with one finger that it was for me. He wanted me to take it.

I was halfway out when I realized what Lucien wanted me to do. I thought I would take it on the way back, but coming from the latrine I couldn't reach it because the SS was watching and thus I had to keep walking. It was taken by someone else. I was facing the opposite direction so I didn't know who took it or when it was taken. Lucien, standing back next to his friend across from me gestured violently with anger.

Going home, one of the girls told us that a French prisoner had given her a gift of bread and hard-boiled eggs. "How did he do that?" everybody asked, "when nobody came near us at our work stations."

"He put it on the divider for me," she said smugly.

Marta came forward. "That's not true," she argued. "I was behind Ebi, and it was meant for Ebi."

"Yeah?" the girl shot back. "You are lying! You are absolutely crazy!" the girl insisted. "It was for *me*!"

"I was behind Ebi. I saw all along that the little guy with the pipe was trying to tell her to take it," Marta continued.

The girl came at Marta to strike her. She stopped short, realizing that Marta was bigger than she was.

The next day, on the cabinet next to my machine, was a beautiful square scarf and a whole loaf of bread. God! Somebody left it there, I thought. I didn't say anything to anyone, except to Marta. "I'm sure that's for you," she said. "Take it!"

I said, "I wouldn't dare!"

Lucien spent more time with his friend facing me than at his own machine. He was pointing again, but when I looked up at the dividing wall, there was nothing there. He became utterly frustrated. He saw that I had no idea of what he was saying.

Pretending it was an accident, he turned over a cabinet next to his friend. With the SS watching, he motioned and pointed at it repeatedly. The SS looked away.

I pointed to my cabinet. Lucien nodded his head up and down. Yes, yes, yes! that's what he meant. He made a sign of the cross, thanking Jesus Christ that I finally understood.

I shook out the scarf, and he laughing and motioning told me to put it on my head. I was scared. I figured that I had better wait and ask the SS woman. But while the SS guard was not looking I tried it on for a second. Lucien smiled widely, took the pipe out of his mouth, and blew a kiss toward me.

Oh, God! if he was so happy, could he know how I felt?

He pointed again at the cabinet. I took out the bread. He nodded again. I crossed my arms on my chest, showing him how happy I was, saying thanks. He motioned that I should eat it. I ate some, gave some to Marta, and the rest I took home to my mother.

The next day I asked Fanny, the SS woman who took us to work, if I could wear the scarf. She said I could. So I went to work the next day wearing the scarf—and promptly became the target of tearing insults, angry accusations and venal envy.

The French prisoners, with their hand signals, tried to show us that the war would be over soon. "Oh, you misinterpreted," some of the girls around our bunk said. "That's impossible. They are prisoners, too. How would they know?"

"Yes," I ventured to observe. "But they are not behind bars like we are."

Later the SS moved closer and watched the Frenchmen from behind. This curtailed their motioning to us as they had done before. Still they signaled us whenever they could, always encouraging us to hang on and maintain hope.

At leat twice a week Lucien put a piece of bread in my cabinet. Sometimes he added a needle, thread, and even a piece of soap. His friend André worked opposite me, and, it turned out, was Fanny's boyfriend. That could be the reason why she was so kind to me and mom.

One Sunday afternoon, while we sat on our bunks—which out of habit we still called shelves—talking with our friends about food, cooking and baking, some dared to suggest that someday we would go home, cook those "good things," and eat until we were full. Another girl promptly suggested that we all shut up because it was making her hungry.

At work, behind the big machines, I was in a world of my own. My imagination took wing. My thoughts flew to fantasy land. I imagined Yosi. He arrived in a high-ranking uniform, picked me out of here and took me home. Sometimes, instead of imagining Yosi doing all that, I daydreamed that it was Dad and that he did the same thing. The harsh realities of this cruel world seemed to be driving my mind further away from them each day, toward silly, childish daydreams and phantom images.

At Christmas I got a slice of cake from Lucien. That gift made me the topic of general conversation through out the barracks. Each bunk buzzed with what I received from Lucien.

Ari, one of the girls opposite me, claimed that I took Lucien away from her, denying her all his gifts. Her two sisters agreed with her. She claimed that she was much prettier than I, and therefore I must have done something to charm him away, because, as she reasoned, the first day that she went to that place it was she to whom he gave a piece of bread.

"You may be prettier than me," I snapped back, "you are certainly much dumber."

After my comment, insult was traded for equal insult. Her two sisters, Gizi and Ella proved themselves to be much better at hurling insults than was Ari. Mother urged me not to let them bother me, and not to talk back. I did anyway, for a while. When the verbal abuse became a daily routine, it was not long before I was past caring.

Marta received a chain with a crucifix. She had told the French that she was not Jewish. She had been taken to the concentration camp with Jews only on the suspicion that she was Jewish. Eagerly she put her gift around her neck; the chain with its crucifix started new troubles. We were all Jewish, and we pleaded with her not to wear the cross around her neck.

"Why did you come here, if you weren't Jewish?" one girl screamed at her.

"I had no choice," Marta responded, continuing to wear her chain and crucifix. Sadly I realized that whenever any one got luckier than the rest, hate herded out of hiding.

During the winter months we were given sweaters by the

factory supervisors. The sweaters helped to keep us warm, but the treacherous road covered with snow and ice made going to and from work without stockings or socks almost unbearable. Without medicine, frostbite brought on severe suffering. Mom tried to warm my feet with her hands. This didn't help much as we were both wet, cold, and hungry.

In an attempt to keep me warm, mom took me into bed with her. The SS, when she discovered us together during the night while checking with her flashlight, poked me and ordered, "*Los! los! los!* back to your own bunk." She might have thought that we were lesbians. She didn't know that we were mother and child. Many situations like that, I am sure, were the source of rumors of lesbianism in the camps. This may have been true in some cases, but it was not general or common for sex was not a powerful force among the prisoners.

In January and February the weather was brutally cold. The occasional snowstorms made walking almost impossible. The Germans had no alternative, if they wanted us to work at the factory, so they took us to work on the train. Fanny would walk with us to the station. Marta and I followed, keeping very close to each other so that we could keep each other warm. The other girls did the same since Fanny didn't make us march in lines or restrained us in any other way.

While we were waiting one day for the train, which was late because of a crippling storm, Fanny acted strangely. She pushed Marta and me toward the edge of the group—farther and farther off by ourselves. We didn't understand. When the train came, she told us to stay put. The rest of the group boarded the coach as we watched. Then, with a single motion of her arms, she shoved Marta and me into the adjacent car. As we entered, to our great surprise, there stood three French prisoners of war: André, her boyfriend; Jacques, who gave Marta the cross and chain; and Lucien. They must have been in on the plan because they were grinning, their smiles spread across their faces. They certainly weren't shocked like we were.

Collectively they showered us with questions: "Where did you come from?" "How long have you been here?" "Where is your family?" and many others. They gave each of us a package of food and spoke kind words not to despair, "The war will be over soon."

Lucien confessed that he had been a newly-wed when he was drafted. Shortly after he was sent into battle he had been captured, and became a prisoner of war. I listened, trying to stay calm, but it was so terribly cold that my teeth chattered. That embarrassed me, but I couldn't help it. Lucien took off his coat, pulled his sweater over his head, and told me to put it on. I looked at Fanny. She motioned for me to put it on. It was way too big, and I must have looked comical, for everyone started to laugh. At least the sweater was warm.

The next day Lucien put a pair of long socks in my cabinet. They were far too big. They barely could be stuffed into my shoes along with my feet. But they kept me warm.

As had been the situation in Plassow, when I walked in to barracks wearing my flowered dress, everybody buzzed, "What have you done? Who gave it to you?" the same thing happened at Augsburg. The four sisters were the most vicious, each attempting to out do the other with insult and insinuation. One suggested that, "By tomorrow you will be wearing his pants!"

"Don't be naive," barked another. "She must have already been in them!"

I started shouting. "You dirty minded bitches!"

"Look who's talking!" they shouted back.

Mother, resting below, pleaded for me not to pay any attention to the girls. "How can you ignore it?" I cried out.

Mother turned to Marta and pleaded with her to stop me.

The sisters harangue continued. "How come you are the one who always gets gifts? Is it only because of your pretty eyes?"

"That's right," snapped Marta.

"I am prettier," screamed Ari.

"That's what *you* think," Marta said quietly.

Gizi suggested, "Let's take a vote."

I started to climb down from my bunk.

"Look! Look how scared she is," Gizzi gloated, "She is running. She is scared of a vote."

"Yes," I sprung back verbally, looking them straight in the eye. "I'm going to the toilet to vomit, and to shit on all of you and your stupid vote!" Laughter echoed throughout the room.

Mother worked in the factory on the compound where we lived. This was fortunate for her as she was not overly exposed to rain, hail, or snow. But the danger from the air raids was getting worse. The raids were more frequent, and, as always, we were locked in our building when the Germans retreated to the safety of their underground shelters.

We worked during Passover, which fell sometime in March. We all made a solemn pledge to show God how thankful we were for being so good to us in this place by keeping to our tradition by not eating any bread. We decided that we would ask the SS if they would give us an extra soup instead. When the French prisoners saw that we ate no lunch and realized why, they baked potatoes and gave them to us at lunchtime—with the permission of our SS captors.

Air raids became daily doses as the year drew to its close. On Sundays we couldn't leave our room. We were locked in. When the bombs fell quite close to us one Sunday afternoon, Fanny came for us and hurried us to the bomb shelter in the basement of our building.

Suddenly bombs fell all around us. Glass broke from the violent shaking of the bombs hitting target. All of a sudden we saw water pouring into the shelter. Although we screamed in panic at first, we collected our wits and discovered the source from which the water gushed. It was a broken pipe. Holding a brace against the pipe we managed to stop most of the water from jetting out.

We were petrified. Sirens were blowing full blast. Bombs were falling ever closer, shaking the building violently. It swayed from side to side as we prayed.

Finally the raid stopped. Many of us were still holding the pipe, but our grips were weak and we were unable to hold it securely as we were pitched around by the shaking of the building. Water collected nearly knee-high.

The door opened. Everybody ran to show the SS what had happened. She dismissed it as unimportant.

The next day we were locked in again. Nobody came to take us to work. There was no food. There were no SS. All we had were locked doors. We began to think that maybe the Germans had been bombed and that all were now dead.

During the continuing air raids those who could sleep, slept. The rest of us prayed.

In the middle of the night Fanny climbed up on my bed,

shook me to wake me, and woke up Marta next to me. She had brought a small package of food from Lucien and a letter. Jacques had also sent Marta a little package and wrote a few words. Now, Fanny declared, she wanted us to write to them to stop them from the insane act they were planning to carry out. "I don't want them to be killed," she said softly. Her ordinarily calm manner had vanished. She was almost pleading.

She handed Marta paper and pencil with a flashlight. "Write them a note," she implored.

"What are they planning, and why?" we asked her. "How can we stop them?"

"Tomorrow morning you will be taken away from here," Fanny said.

We gasped.

"Sh-sh!" she cautioned.

"Where are we going?"

"Back to Dachau," Fanny whispered.

"Why?"

"Because everything is bombed out here."

"Oh, my God!"

Again she "sh-sh"-ed us to be quiet.

"In the command bunker everybody died," Fanny told us. "But there are still many SS in the area."

Fanny paused. "When I told them that you would all be taken away, when I told Andre, they swore to protest, and they theatened to march in front of the train. They'll be shot if they do that. So write a note to them and tell them that you don't want them to do that."

We wrote as we were told, but in the morning, as we marched to the station, there they were: Lucien and Jacques, shouting and screaming in French, showing signs of victory with their hands.

We were ushered into the boxcars again. The SS bolted the doors, locking out the sight of the two brave Frenchmen.

The note from Lucien to me, which I had Marta read to me over and over, was quickly engraved into my heart. He wrote:

> Your presence brought sunshine into my life. I ad-
> mire your courage. Please keep it up. No matter
> what hardships, always remember, my prayers

will be following you wherever you are, and the war
will be over soon. We are very close to the end of
the war, and when it is over, I will look and hope to
find you. Keep those big beautiful eyes shining, and
remember my address: 19 Rue Grill, LeHarve,
France, where my wife and I will be waiting with
open doors, open hearts, and open arms.

First Fanny, then Marta, and then mother begged me to
destroy the letter. I refused. I stuck it in my bosom and carried
it with me. The other girls didn't know about the letter, but
some saw Fanny during the night and wondered why she was up
there on my bunk.

The nightmare of Nazism is only suggested by these
piles of bodies at the concentration camp at Belsen,
Germany. These victims died of disease and starvation,
but millions more—men, women, and children—were
deliberately murdered.

Barna Grünblatt

1945

Chapter Ten

Muhldorf—March 1945

This time we were over 80 people in the box car, all wondering where we were to be railroaded. "To Dachua," I said.

"Where is that?"

Nobody knew.

In a few hours we arrived. Again we were lined up in rows of five. We were marched up the to camp gate, where we were forced to stand waiting for two or three hours. Then we were turned around and marched back to the train. Fanny, who had come with us, whispered, "No room."

We were ordered back into the box cars. "Now we are going to Muhldorf," Fanny told us as we boarded. No one had heard of that place either, but by morning we arrived and were marched into the camp.

Like at Dachau, we were not expected here. Again we were marched away to different destinations: ten or twenty girls at a time. The dividing line did not separate me from Mom, but one did come between Marta and me as the SS marched her away.

For hours we stood there. I cried and begged to see the *lagerelteste* (the head of the camp), to ask her where they had taken my friend Marta.

"Oh," the camp head responded. "She was taken five miles from here to another camp, called Waldlager."

"Please, take me also to that place," I begged.

"How do you know what will be there? How do you know if it will be better, or worse? than here."

"I want to be with my friend," I continued. "I need her. She is the only interpreter who can communicate for me."

"Okay," responded the *lagerelteste*. "Let me see."

She came back soon, took two rows, gave us over to an SS soldier, and then had the ten of us march through the *Wald* (or forest), to the *Waldlager* (forest camp). When we arrived at the camp it appeared that there were only men. We were then taken to the end of the camp, to a fenced-in barracks. Some girls were there, including Marta. We hugged and kissed. I explained how I had begged to be with her.

Within minutes, a mass of living skeletons gathered at the wire. They looked like the ones we saw at Plassow. They were congregating, looking for relatives. Some of them were the same foreign speaking girls that we had seen in Plassow, so we knew that there were Polish people among them.

The *capos* asked who could write German. I volunteered and became the *Schreiberin*. My only function was to write on a piece of paper how many girls went to work each day from my small barracks; that was all that I had to do.

A man who was not wearing a striped uniform and was not so terribly skeletal came to the wire one day. He wanted to know where we were from, and if there were any Polish women among us. I motioned him toward some other women, but he came back and told me that they were not Polish, but Czech. I did not understand the rest of what he asked. He stood there for a moment and then motioned for me to wait, indicating that he would be right back.

The man returned with an interpreter. Through the interpeter the man asked me if I was with any girls from the Polish city of Lodz. I responded that I did not know. He then asked me how old I was, where I came from, and the routine questions we were all familiar with, especially "How long have you been here?"

He asked if I was hungry. I shook my head no. Marta was behind me, and retorted, "Are you crazy? How can you say that you are not hungry?" I was too embarrassed to admit it. I don't know why I was so embarrased.

The interpreter said to me, "Don't be silly. Don't say that. Everybody is starving to death."

The man I did not understand reached into his pocket and took out a piece of bread. I told Marta, "If he throws it here, you pick it up. I will split it with you. I just can't put my hand out and ask him for it."

The man threw the bit of bread over the fence. Marta picked it up. I shared it with her. The man watched, and said nothing.

He was back the next day. He stood in the same place.

He was of average height with a couple month's fuzz on his head, as we all did. He had green eyes and an oval face with beautiful, perfectly matched teeth, and equally perfect formed lips that gave him a handsome appearance. He wore a wine-colored sweater that made him even more outstanding among the raggedly dressed wretches of the camp.

I did not know who he was, nor how he could preserve himself so well. I only knew that he was Polish, and that his name was Salek. Every morning, when I looked out the window from our bunker-like barracks, he stood there at the fence, staring, just staring. Each time I looked over, our eyes met. Soon we began to smile at each other.

He wanted to talk to me. He had a million questions he begged to ask me. He could not as we had no common language between us.

I wondered how long he had been there, because the *capos* didn't look as good as he appeared. Marta and I suggested that he must be in some kind of special position to be dressed like he was. I told her how he stayed all day, watching, and when I came out he would get closer to the wire (which was not electrified), and with his hand constantly motioning for me to come closer.

"You idiot!" Marta exclaimed, "why don't you go there? He probably wants to give you something!"

I said that I didn't want to take anything from him. "He is not like Lucien who can buy whatever he pleases. This man is in the same boat that we are in."

"Are you crazy? Don't you see how good he looks? He surely has more than we have!"

Salek just watched from the fence.

After roll call and our soup, which looked and tasted as if it had come straight from Auschwitz or Plassow, Salek appeared by the wire again. He held in one hand two slices of bread and one cooked potato. In the other, motioning me with it, he held a sweater. I cried out, "Wait! I'll call my friend."

"*Nein! Nein!*" he shouted, shaking his head. "For you! for you!" He pointed at me.

I tried to explain in sign language that half of the food I wanted to give to my friend. He signaled back, no, that's all for you. He made circles with his hand: all for you, and then he wrapped everything in the sweater and threw it over the fence.

Other girls ran toward it. He shouted at them, "Leave it alone! It's for her!"

I picked up the sweater and its precious contents and went to the fence to thank him. He had the most beautiful smile with those even teeth. He wanted me to eat everything right away in front of him, but I waited for mother who was still working.

When mom came back and saw me at the fence she walked over. We hugged and kissed each other and I handed her a slice of bread, explaining that it was from Salek. I tried to give her half of the potatoes, but she attempted to force them into my mouth instead.

Salek watched as she forced me to eat. Suddenly he took his hands from his pockets, where he had hidden them all the time. He raised them to his cheeks in a look of amazement.

"*Acht der leiber!*" he exclaimed as if he had just discovered something unbelievable. With his hand he urged me to come closer to the fence. Still with a million questions on his face, he pointed at mom, whispering, "*Mutter? mutter?*"

Mom was 44 years old. She looked 34. I shook my head yes. He was genuinely overjoyed. I hadn't seen anything like it since I left home.

The next morning he watched where mother went to work, walking up the line with her. He asked her in Yiddish if she was my mother. Mom smiled yes. He pushed a package into her hand.

When mom came from work and told me what happened, I asked her "How could you take it from him? Maybe he meant if for somebody else."

Mom looked very serious for a moment. Then she explained to me, "He asked if I was your mother. I am, am I not? I am a mother, yours for sure."

After roll call he came back to the wire with a skeleton-looking young boy in a striped uniform. The youth interpreted for the man, talking in Hungarian, "Please," the boy began. "talk to this Polish man. He said he will give me an extra *zulag* (meaning, poriton) if you talk with him. Please. I am so very hungry."

I responded quickly. "Okay. But I cannot speak German."

"He can speak four or five languages," he told me. I shrugged, "I can only speak Hungarian."

"Only Hungarian?" the boy cried with dismay.

"Don't worry," I said. "Tell him that I will talk with him, if not with anything else, with my hands and with my eyes."

A round-faced, dark-complexioned man also dressed in civilian clothes like Salek stood a few feet away observing our unusual conversation. Unexpectedly, he walked over to Salek and tried to push him, but Salek stopped him, asking him in German what he wanted.

"You talked enough with her already. Now it's my turn." He moved directly in front of Salek.

"But I don't want to talk to him," I told the youth.

Salek and the other man conversed in French. Then they began to push each other.

The boy explained to me that the new one was a *Blockelteste*, the head of the block for the adjacent men's barracks, and that he was a Greek. "He will give me the same extra portion," the youth explained, "if you talk to him."

"Okay," I replied. "But I don't speak French or Greek."

"Spanish?"

"I can't."

"I know, I know; you speak only Hungarian."

"That's right," I confirmed. I felt like a complete idiot.

The two men stood there, Salek and the Greek. Both asked the boy, "What did she say? What did she say?"

The youth told them that I was willing to talk to both of them. At that the Greek, whose name was Hayim, jumped up, waving his hands, crying, "No! no! no!" He was determined that I should talk only to him.

"Tell him he is crazy," I sputtered. "I talk to everybody."

The poor little interpreter almost cried. For a minute there, he had a chance at extra slices of bread and a portion of soup from both Salek and from Hayim. Now I had refused to talk to one of them, he thought.

Salek saw the boy's despair. He promised the youth two portions.

Salek must have been important, I thought, because in the package he gave him there was a boiled egg, margarine, and about twenty saccharines. It was the first time I really had a sweet coffee and some bread and hard boiled eggs for a long time. And once again I became the topic of conversation, not only in my barracks, but in the other four blocks as well. Hayim would dig a little ditch under the wire to push through a *men-*

aske of baked potatoes. I would spend the evening defending myself. I was considered by many to be the Greek's girlfriend, but when Salek was seen giving me something, I was considered his girlfriend.

Another Polish boy, who worked in the carpentry shop, made me a little wooden box. The girls in our barracks asked me where I got the treasure box. Again their insinuations and crass comments.

I cried easily. In fact I was on the verge of tears all the time. Alfonse, the head of the Lager, asked me when I handed him the daily work roster, "What's the matter with you, little one? You always cry."

I showed with hand motions how the girls were always talking about me.

He smiled. "Don't pay any attention to them."

"How can I ignore their lies?"

"Simple," he said, and covered his ears with his hands. "Like this."

I yearned and daydreamed for times that never came, for times that never were, and for the times behind the huge machines at Augsburg which, I looked back on, were safer the times that existed in this compound.

Mother talked with Salek in her limited Yiddish. Because of her skills in Yiddish, mom became my official interpreter for him.

As April 1945 came, we marked that we had been at the Waldlager camp for three weeks. We could hear chaos and screaming every day coming from the center of the camp—a place we never went. The women were always locked in unless they were at work. I had no other job and so I never left the barrack's fenced enclosure.

Salek came to the fence every day. There he stood with his hands in his pockets, watching my barracks. Every day he brought me a little soup, or a little slice of bread. We communicated as best we could. He tried to tell me that the war would be over soon. He knew that all his family had been killed by the Nazis. His father had been a textile manufacturer in Lodz, and therefore he was the first to be killed in the ghetto. His mother and one brother died in the gas chambers at Auschwitz; they had been the first Jews to be taken there. His second brother was taken to Treblinka, Poland, where he was murdered in the Nazi gas chamber. Now he was alone. There was nothing to go home to.

I felt so sorry for him. "Maybe you're mistaken," I offered. "Maybe they are all still alive." His eyes became misty. I wanted so badly to change his train of thought. I didn't want him to be so depressed. But my ability was limited by my language barrier and thus all I could do was attempt to make him understand, using my hands and my eyes.

He gave me encouragement, too, lifting my spirits daily with his visits, his assurances that we would be free soon, and with his small parcels of food. He smiled at my helplessness in trying to talk to him. I struggled to tell him about the malicious rumors, and he laughed when he finally understood.

Salek called mom over. In Yiddish, and with hand motions he said, "Tell her with all the death and destruction around us, why does she bother? Why is she concerned with wagging tongues?"

One afternoon, in our third week there, the chaos from the center of the camp exploded, and like wild animals the men broke into our area, shouting, "We are free! We are free!"

Salek broke through and pulled me away from the masses of men swarming over everything and everyone. I don't remember there being anyone smaller than me, and I could easily have been run over. Salek hoisted me to safety.

Hayim came with Dario, another Greek, and pushed Salek aside. Pointing with his index finger, almost touching my nose, he asked, "Will it be me? Or, will it be him?"

I had no idea what he was asking me. Mother was edging herself closer to find out what he wanted. Dario explained using the same limited Yiddish that my mother commanded, that Hayim was asking who I wanted to talk to, Salek or him? Hayim wanted me to be his girl.

I told mother to tell him not to be stupid. "What does he mean, his girl? I never saw him before! I have had nothing to do with him. He gave me a little bit of food, but that doesn't mean that I will consent to be his girlfriend."

"So what is Salek doing here?" he wanted to know.

"The same as with Hayim," I said. The two Greeks picked up Salek and shoved him aside. Hayim repeated that he wanted to talk to me. As he started to step closer, the whole camp erupted in gunfire. Machines were blasting on all sides of us. Everyone ran.

The freedom that had been shouted into the air moments ago had been an illusion. The shooting continued for almost an hour. The Germans were quickly re-establishing control over the camp. But we had had the sensation, even if it was only momentary, that we were a free people. It gave us hope and belief that eventually liberation would come. These were the last moments of our enslavement. We must survive them!

We took cover from the machine guns that were firing without pause, while above the sky was crowded with Allied airplanes. Bombs were exploding nearby and everywhere.

The Germans were firing from the watchtowers at any prisoners who were attempting to run, or even those who were making a motion about to run. They weren't running to escape now, only to take cover from the bombs. Machine gun bullets were cutting them down everywhere.

When the shooting subsided, SS appeared and ordered us out of the barracks. They commanded us to form into rows of five. "*Los! los! los!*" they shouted.

I ran into formation. Mother was right behind me, just coming out of the door of our barracks. I motioned to her that we had to go. She grabbed the dress and the little wooden box and ran to join us in the quickly formed rows of fives.

We were ordered to march—the entire camp was to march at once. Women were in the front of the march. Men were behind. "*Los! los! los!*—faster, faster, faster," the SS barked. It looked like the SS were attempting to empty the camp. I had never seen so many SS in one place.

We had been marching about ten minutes when I heard my name called, "Ebi! Ebi!" I stepped out of line and looked back. In a long winter coat, package in hand, Salek came running forward. The SS in charge of the marching men must have known him, I thought, because nobody bothered him. He joined our part of the line and stayed next to me, the only man walking with the women. Out of breath, he was trying to tell us that his *Stubenfierer* wanted him to stay with a small detachment remaining at the camp, but that he wanted to come with me.

"Tell him," I said to mother, "that he is very unwise, because the women are separated anyway, no matter where they take us, and we don't know where we are going. Here, at least, he has a chance to save his life."

Salek told mom that he didn't care as long as he stayed next to me.

"Oh," I gasped, "tell him that he is as crazy as Hayim." I looked at him. Although I smiled I shook my head with disapproval.

After some hours of marching we were ordered on to box cars again. They were already filled with prisoners, sitting and standing in whatever space there was. When our group was crammed in, we were over one hundred women in one car. Many were screaming in Polish. We must have stepped on numerous hands and feet struggling to get in.

The next ten days were the pinnacle of our horror. We were supposed to be destroyed in the Alps at Garmisch. They had managed to take the last few box cars, but they didn't have time to take us all because the railroad in which we were pushed back and forth was partially bombed.

The Nazis stopped the train and opened the door only after two days and two nights. One more day, we thought, and those who didn't die would have gone insane.

Mother resumed her imaginary discoveries of fresh air "gushing in" through the tiny opening high on the box car wall. "Look! look! look! Breathe! Breathe!" she kept telling me, until she herself turned blue from lack of oxygen.

When the door opened, people half dead fell out on to the ground. From outside the box car came shouts of "Ebi! Ebi!" I made my way close enough to the open door to look. There was Salek. He jumped up into the box car, opened his shirt, and spilled out loaf after loaf of hot, freshly baked bread! As it fell, a hundred hands grabbed for it, almost pulling him down, too.

"Please," he begged, pointing to me, "Just for her." The crazed skeletons were too starved to listen. They were too busy devouring the feast that fell in their laps. Salek's whole upper body was red from the burns of the hot bread that he had stolen. He had gotten the chance by being one of the influential prisoners selected for a special work detail.

Mother and I grieved over our loss. Salek gestured for us not to despair. He said that he would be right back. And soon he was—with potatoes. He held them high over his head until he could reach us. Then, with one hand, he guided a potato into my mouth, and with the other hand he fed the second potato to my mother. He stayed, guarding us while we ate, then kissed our cheeks and jumped off.

Before they closed the box cars, Alfonse, the head of the Lager and now in charge of the group during the transport, came looking for me. He found me and, while others cursed, handed me a half a loaf of bread "that Salek sends". He said, "Eat this while I stand here. I want you to eat it all right now." I ate half of it, and put the other half in my bosom, tell him that the rest was for my mother.

"Who? What did you say?"

"I said 'my mother'." I pointed her out to him. He said that he had no idea. "You have done well in keeping it secret."

I broke off pieces of the bread and fed mother without risking trying to hand it to her. The women around us were grabbing at it, coming within inches of snatching it from my hand.

Hayim showed up, too, with four potatoes. He stood outside, calling, "Come here! Come here!"

I wouldn't crawl over all of those people to get to the open door. Everybody was reaching and pleading for the food they saw him hold. "Are those Pollacks in there?" Hayim asked.

I nodded my head yes.

He got angry, threw the potatoes in the door, and left. The potatoes vanished in a scramble of starving bodies. We never got near them.

The moaning, the crying, the screaming, became louder as they closed the door on us and the train began to move. All ranting in different languages, most of them bony with eyes bulging, the box car looked like an overcrowded insane asylum. The smell was suffocating.

Rows of box cars longer than any I had seen, now held thousands of displaced people. Most of them had been caged in the box cars for days. They had no food. They had no water. Hysteria was raging.

On the third day the train stopped. The door opened. Before I could get to it, Salek was calling out, "Ebi! Ebi!" He helped me down over a mass of bodies. Then he helped mom down. He grabbed our hands, and told mom that we were free and to run. Not only did we run, but hundreds of others ran through the forested German countryside. Salek pulled me with one hand, and with his other hand he pulled mom along, as she grasped the little chest with the spare dress tighter under her arm. Salek suggested that she should abandon it so that we could run faster. But mom held on to it. She wouldn't let it go.

The terrain was tough. We stumbled and fell. Salek took off his topcoat and threw it away.

Petrified, mom asked, "What did you do that for?"

"It's too heavy. I can't run in it," Salek explained.

"But if we are free, as you say, why do we have to run?"

"Because everybody else is running," he said to mom, who was still talking, interpreting for me while stumbling across the forest floor at the same time.

Salek again told her that the extra weight was holding us back. He grabbed everything that we had and threw it away, extra clothing included, and then grabbed our hands and kept running. "Don't worry about those things," he said. "When we get home, or when we get totally free, we're going to get all those things back. Just *run!*"

Mother cried out that she had to stop. "I don't want to run anymore," she said. "If we are free, it's fine. Then we don't have to run. And if we are not free, I don't want to be a fugitive for I can't go any further."

Machine gun fire sounded suddenly from every direction.

"Don't stop now! Don't stop now!" Salek urged us to go on. "Just a little more until we get into the woods!"

We reached a dense growth of trees, away from the bullets. "What was that? Why were they shooting?"

Salek shrugged. He didn't know either.

"Then how come they told you that we are free, and who told you that we are free?" mom asked.

"Well," he said, "when the SS opened the box car they had said, 'everyone can go. You are free'."

Mother asked again. "Then why are they shooting at us?"

Salek admitted that it was a puzzle to him, too, "But for the time it is best that we stay in the woods and wait."

Within an hour we heard more noises. Salek went to investigate. He came back and said that a large group of people were

were near by. "It's best that we join them," he said.

When we did, we realized that German soldiers were guarding them on three sides to prevent any further escape. It was an awfully big crowd.

When we saw the SS we panicked. "Don't worry," Salek said. He smiled, trying to show confidence.

The SS ordered the men and women to separate again in groups. Salek constantly looked in my direction, smiling, trying to reassure me that we were going to survive, to live, and to be free.

We were near some kind of farm where we could see the SS stabbing stacks of hay with their bayonets, looking for other fugitives. To control us futher the SS shoved us into a ditch, ordering us to kneel and place our hands on our heads. Mom whispered, like Salek, "Don't get scared."

How ironic. Here we were, kneeling in a ditch, our arms reaching to the sky, telling each other not to be afraid. I wasn't frightened—I was paralyzed. I looked in Salek's direction. The men had their backs to us, but were in the same position: kneeling, hands held up high. The soldiers were in front of them, pointing their guns at them as they were pointing their guns at us. They questioned us, asking what we were going to do and where we were going. Salek became the spokesman. He reported that when the SS opened the box cars, they had told the prisoners that they were free to go. "So we went, but soon we heard the shooting. We were afraid to turn back because of the shooting. We were afraid of the bullets. That's why we are here."

The SS declared that if Salek was telling the truth we would not be harmed, "But we are going to check the story."

Soldiers were dispatched to retrace our steps, to see if there was a train nearby.

It was a long, agonizing wait. The SS formed us into close, very tight groups, no longer were we marched in rows of fives. Salek helped and held on to mother as they marched us forward whispering to her words that I could not understand. Later she told me that she could not understand much of what he said either.

It was dark when we got back to the box cars. Still I could see dead men and women lying everywhere. Some had been shot. Others were dead from starvation. Many were still barely alive as I could see them move or hear them moan. Salek grabbed my arm and pushed me forward, pulling mother with his other hand. He in German, and mother in Hungarian, instructed me, "Don't look. Just don't look. Go straight ahead. Don't look at anything." He pushed me into the first box car we came to. Then he helped mom to get in, and finally jumped in behind us.

People stood all around. The SS stood nearby, talking among themselves. Salek made room for us, then for himself and sat down. "You see?" he said, "Nothing to be afraid of."

"What is he saying?" I asked my mother.

Each time he waited patiently while mom interpreted. When I would get impatient, he would just smile—no matter what horror was going on around us.

Chaos was everywhere. Outside the box car pandemonium broke loose. The train didn't move. The Germans had nowhere to take us. Inside the box car we were hungry, thirsty, tired and terrified. People all around us were dying. When starvation claimed another victim, someone would scream in the dark, "Help! Somebody just fell on me! Help me!" Everybody tried to free the one who was still alive from the heavy mantle of a wretched cadaver which had once held life.

At around midnight the Germans shoved everybody in—men and women together. But still there was no more room than there had been in the forenoon. With mom in the middle, Salek on one side, and I on the other, we leaned against the box car wall and fell asleep.

**Salek & Ebi,
July 26, 1945**

Three months after
liberation.

Chapter Eleven

Liberation–April 30, 1945

In the morning the SS opened the doors, told everybody to get out and separated the men and the women. Men were assigned to find the dead and stack them "in neat piles." The women were marched toward the middle of a huge line of box cars, and started piling us in.

I lost sight of Salek. I didn't know where he was. The train moved forward. We settled ourselves down, and noticed that again, instead of a hundred people in the box car, we were only about seventy. We were relieved to have a little more room.

The train moved ahead, for how long we lost track. Then it moved backward. How far we were from where we had been—how far we were from Salek—mom and I had no idea.

Early in the morning a loud terrifying air raid began. It was heard in every direction. The planes came over so low that they seemed to be just above our heads. The machine guns sounded as if they were just outside the box car walls—rat-tat-tat-tat-tat. Then they stopped.

The SS opened our doors and directed us to get beneath the box cars. Mom and I were scared to move. We sat there as our car emptied. A line of box cars moving on the track beside us stopped. The doors opened. People spilled out. Many fell to the ground dead.

The planes came back. We could see them out of the open box car door. They came from all directions. They looked close enough for us to touch. Then, in a split second, they shot up in to the sky and disappeared.

By noon the ground was strewn with the dead and wounded as the Germans let the prisoners stay where they fell. Greek prisoners from nearby box cars came by ours checking for casualties and ordering us to take cover. "What's the use?" I started to say, but they lifted mother and me out through the door and shoved us under the box car.

We lay stretched out flat on the ground, motionless, until the raid ended. We saw Alfonse stumbling along next to the train, trying to keep track of the people. He told me that Hayim had run away during the false liberation the day before. He just hoped that Hayim hadn't been shot somewhere.

We were ordered back into the boxcars by the SS who told us that we would get some food during the day. After three days, that was the best news they could have given us.

Then came that urgent, welcome cry, "Ebi! Ebi!" It was Salek.

Immediately he was by our side. He broke off chunks of bread from a whole loaf, pushing it into my mother's mouth and into mine.

Everybody around us begged for some of the bread. Salek shook his head no. "Not this time. You won't take it this time."

"Just a little bit," they pleaded. Salek handed out a few small pieces.

We were sitting against the box car wall, relishing our feast. Suddenly there was another air raid. Bullets were flying from what seemed like a million planes at once. Planes were attacking at eye level. We could see smoke from their guns and the rat-tat-tat-tat was the loudest ever.

Salek ordered me down. Everybody was already down. At least I could breathe if I stayed sitting up, I thought. Salek grabbed me, and threw me down on top of people already lying flat on the box car floor. At that moment a bullet whistled through the wall precisely where I had been sitting and hit a girl who sat opposite me in the box car. It went between her eyes. Her sister saw her slump dead next to her and jumped at me screaming, "It's your fault! You killed my sister!" She was clawing at me, but before she could reach me Salek grabbed her arms.

"Calm yourself," he said pulling her down next to me, "Come on, sit down here. How can it be Ebi's fault. I am sorry for you and your sister, but it's not Ebi's fault."

"Yes!" she kept screaming, trying to free herself from his grip. "Yes it is!"

"If she hadn't gotten out of that seat, then the bullet would not have come and killed my sister. I will kill you for that!" she said, shaking her finger at me. "I swear I will kill you!"

She repeated her threat over and over. Her voice was soon drowned out by more shooting.

Now the raids were non-stop. The Germans didn't know

what to do with us. Nor did they know what to do with themselves. They locked the box car door. Then they opened the door. The hurried to clear away our dead. Disposing of their victims' bodies became extremely important to them as the Allies advanced. This is what finally saved our lives. If they killed us now, thousands and thousands of our bodies would bear winess to their deed.

After the last air raid, some prisoners took their striped uniforms off and spread them out on the tops of the box cars, hoping that the Allied pilots would see them there and not attack us. Whether for that reason or by the grace of God, we were not attacked again by the planes.

We were locked in again after the dead were removed. The train moved forward. Just as quickly it stopped. We heard gunshots both in the distance and very near. Was it the Germans killing Jews, or was it the Allies advancing?

We prayed, those who still believed, to God. We prayed for the English and the Americans to come, please, anybody, to save us. We struggled now as never before. Each of us fought a private war of will over despair. We felt as if we were neither dead nor alive, and we wanted it to be one way or the other. To live meant we needed food and water, and we cried out for that. But to live also meant an existence no human being was ever meant to share. The box cars were testimony to that.

The decaying corpses were still inside. Despite the Germans' last efforts to hide their crimes against humanity, there were still hundreds of corpses riding with us. Living relatives had covered them from view so as to spend an extra day with them, not realizing that it might have been more than a day before the doors would be opened again, and that, in the meantime, the smell would suffocate us and could kill us.

The guns sounded very close. Then we heard something that sounded like a tank. This gave us new hope. Maybe one more day, or one more hour and it would be over. We summonded the will.

The door opened. Those leaning against it practically fell out. We pushed the stinking bodies to the front of the car, relatives screaming, "Careful! careful!" as if their loved ones were still alive.

Those able to move jumped out to the fresh air. I pulled

mom with me. Outside there were dead everywhere.

A German SS soldier, with his jacket off, having no gun, no hat, sat at the opening of our box car. "I saved you from being shot like these people who were in the first box car," he said. "Now I ask that you save me."

We just stared at him. "You are free," he kept saying to us. We looked at him dumbfounded. We had been through too much in the last few days to react to anything quickly.

Again the SS soldier said, "You must save me." He pointed down the road. "Those are the Americans. The Americans."

The holocaust survivors, some still sitting in the doorway of the box car shouted. Others cried. Some prayed. Many exclaimed, "We are free! We are free!"

The living jumped over the dead and half-dead. Hugging and kissing, they fell on each other overwhelmed with joy. It was April 30, 1945.

In ten minutes Salek came running towards me with a bunch of wildflowers in his hand. He hugged me and kissed me, and he hugged and kissed mom. Then he hugged and kissed me again. He lifted me up and down, shouting, "We finally are free!"

He pulled me excitedly to an embankment where the American tanks were passing. Soldiers riding in the tanks threw us little packages of cheese and crackers.

We caught some of the packages, broke them open and ate what was inside. It was, and remains, the greatest feast of the finest food that I have ever eaten.

God bless those soldiers! I wondered, so many times, who they were and where they are now.

We were on the railroad tracks between Munich and Garmisch Partenkirchen, near the little town of Tutzing. It would be in this little town that we would later be officially liberated.

Within minutes the American soldiers were everywhere, collecting the dead, and running with stretchers to carry the sick. They told us to stay put. They promised to bring food for everybody. "Soon, soon, soon," the pledged. They said they hadn't expected to find so many starved people.

The Americans picked up the Germans. They asked us to identify the German soldiers—many of whom had removed their uniforms, stripped dead prisoners of their clothing and put on the prison stripes themselves in an effort to avoid detection. But the German SS were healthy, well-fed men. That was obvious to the Americans who were quickly taking the dead and the sick, and even the Germans, away in different directions. To each of us they handed out bread and cheese.

Hysterically everyone reached for the food at the same time with the stronger pushing the weak away. The Americans pleaded for calm, trying to explain that there was enough for everybody, but the desperate skeletons did not understand English. Seeing food, they lunged for it.

We were lined up according to box car. This caused hundreds to claim that theirs was the first box car.

Salek disappeared. In a few minutes he was back with a portion of bread and cheese.

Some girls recognized me. They shouted, "Here, too? Is she the privileged one, here too?"

Now they didn't bother me. They couldn't bother me ever again. I had become immunized against their malicious innuendoes.

Within an hour the fast-moving Americans had fed us, having taken us in trucks to Feldafing, a Hitler youth training camp vacated by the Germans as the Americans approached. It was a fully equipped army base where the elite youth of Germany were trained. Inside its huge dwelling buildings, double layer bunk beds with white sheets and white pillow cases and neatly laid out blankets awaited us.

Everybody shouted! "Look! look! White sheets!" Some immediately laid on them to see if they were real.

I went with mom from room to room, and found that every bed was taken by girls who sat on them, claiming them as their own.

I opened the door to a small office. There was a couch inside. "Look mom, this is our room! All by itself! We won't let anybody come in. Our place. All our own!" I told her I would get sheets and pillows and sleep on the couch or floor, but this would be all ours.

The Allied soldiers told us that we would take showers a barracks at a time. There was plenty of room, therefore, we were asked, not to run, not to push, and not to take or grab anything as "there is plenty of everything for everybody."

At the showers we were handed a bar of soap and a huge bath towel. We were told we could keep both.

Nobody wanted to get out from under the first hot water we had felt since we left home. We wanted it to last forever. But a voice on the loudspeaker asked us to "please, move on." The voice said that we would shower again tomorrow, and "please, let others bathe, also," and "do so quickly so that the hot food won't get cold waiting " for us to come.

"Please, don't take more than one towel. Leave the rest for the others," the loudspeaker continued, as we piled towel upon towel upon towel to take with us.

On the way out we were handed Hitler Youth uniform pajamas and ordered to the mess hall. There we each received a plate of the most unique and fabulous food we had eaten to date. It was a mixture of meat, potatoes, and vegetables: like a stew. We shouted to each other out of excitement and joy, comparing this delicious stew to the watery soup that we had eaten for such a long time, throughout our captivity.

In the middle of our excitement, Salek came to the mess hall looking for me. Mother had gone to the kitchen to help prepare the food for the next group.

I had a hard time communicating with Salek. All I could do was kiss him and smile.

We sat in the mess hall until mom was through. She said she was asked to come back the next day to help. She had responded, she told us, "It would be a pleasure."

For ten days all we had to wear was pajamas. After each shower we got a clean pair. Those who fit into them got a Hitlerjugend uniform, but clothes for all 30,000 liberated men and women were not available.

The next morning the Americans gave us 24 hours to do as we wanted to do. Some set out to steal whatever they could. Some set out in search of revenge. Salek and I sat on the couch and hugged and kissed while mom prepared a breakfast of the cheese and bread Salek had stolen earlier.

Life in the DP camp is another story. But by the ironies of life, and the twists of fate, the girl who gave me the hardest time in Augsburg asked me to be her witness at a marriage to one of the Polish prisoners, a man who was Salek's best friend. We were all in Hitlerjugend uniforms as our friends were.

The couple was married by a justice of the peace. They married five weeks after they had been liberated.

After they had been pronounced man and wife, they turned to us. Smiling they asked, "How about you two doing the same, and we'll be your witnesses!"

We all laughed. Moments later, on June 12, 1945, Salek and I became man and wife.

Ebi Gabor (1987)

Epilogue

Los Angeles, California—July 1985

Mor Grünblatt died in Auschwitz. He died in the gas chamber moments after he bid his family goodbye on May 22, 1944. Laci Grünblatt, Ebi's eldest brother, died in a Soviet prison camp in Siberia in 1942.

Tibi Grünblatt, Ebi's next eldest brother, survived his imprisonment in a Nazi slave labor camp in Hungary. He died in Los Angeles in 1978.

Barna Grünblatt, the last of the Ebi's three brothers, lives in Dallas, Texas. There he pursues his career as an electronics engineer.

Ebi's grandparents, six of her aunts, and sixteen of her cousins all perished at Auschwitz.

Jassi Farago survived the Nazi slave labor imprisonment. He died in Canada in 1967.

Lucien La Fabre died in a motor vehicle accident in Germany on April 30, 1945, the day of his liberation as a prisoner of war.

Hayim is a successful businessman in Tel Aviv, Israel.

The American soldier who tossed the packet of cheese and crackers that Ebi caught on liberation day vanished down the road in his tank. Ebi is still trying to find him to thank him.

Salek Monitz is a successful businessman in Los Angeles, California. Today his name is Richard Monitz.

Margaret Grünblatt and her daughter Ebi are still together. They live in Los Angeles, Calfiornia.

SS Officer Hans Kundi lives in Hamburg, Germany.

Marta Juranyi lives in Winnipeg, British Columbia, Canada.

INDEX

Allied air raids 179, 190, 197f
Allied forces. 201, 202
American soldiers 199f
Amosninos, Hayim . .187-189, 192
Arrow Cross (Hungarian) 1, 3
. . . . . .15f, 26, 29, 31f, 58, 59
Augsburg. 169f
Auschwitz . . . . .viii, 30, 71-97, 99
. . . . 161-168
barter in camps. 46
Birkenau . . . . .viii, 163f
Blockowa, authority of. 91-93
capos power of 159
Christian political prisoners. . . 116
. . . . 176
Dachau 180, 183
Debrecen. 2, 13, 30
Entlausung. 94, 107, 133, 138
. . . . 165
Farago, Yosi. 48-56
Feldafing (Nazi youth camp)
. . . . 201-203
frau auseherin. 172f
Garmisch. 191
German population reaction to
forced labor of Jews. 171
Grunblatt, Barna. 1, 8, 11, 15
. . . . 16, 19, 55, 58, 68, 75
. . . . 85, 163
Grunblatt, Ebi *passim*
Grunblatt, Laci. 3
Grunblatt, Margaret (Margit)
(mother of Ebi) *passim*
Grunblatt, Mor(ris, father of
Ebi) 1-75, 84, 85
Grunblatt, Tibor (Tibi) 2, 3
. . . . 31, 32
insanity. 67
Jews
arrest of Hungarian . . 10, 23-25
Christian attitude toward abuse
of. 23-24
cremation of, in camps. 87
Czech 38, 118f

Jews (*continued*)
deportation of 11, 13f
forced marches of . . .22-23 sqq.
ghettoization of 11-12, 25
. . . . 36f, 54f
humiliation of, based of physical
characteristic (circumcision) .3
. . . . .4, 43, 45, 79-81
among religious. 79ff
beards and 54ff
mass marriage of 48f
planned liquidation of by
Nazis. 39, 101-102, 189
Polish 77, 92, 96f, 102-103
. . . . .119, 184f, 192f
separation of families. . . .72-76
theft of property of 4-9
transportation of. . .57-70, 196f
K.U.K.A. Ammunition Factory
. . . . 170-173ff
Krankenhaus 90, 148-151
LaFabre, Lucien .174-178, 180-181
lesbianism, fear of 177
Mengele, Josef . . .vii, 76-77, 95-97
. . . . 100, 162, 167-168
Monitz, Salek . . .184-187, 189-204
Muhldorf. 183f
Nyiregyhaza & Nazis 35, 59
Passover. 16
Plassow as Nazi camp. 99-160
Rockommando 117, 118, 131
. . . . .138, 152-153
SS, use of dogs . . .76-79, 118, 124
Star of David as symbol 13
suicide by Jews. 164
tattooing in concentration
camps. 164f
Temple, used as human ware-
house in Hungary 11, 12
. 15-21
torture of Jews 155, 158f
triangles, as symbols worn by
prisoners 117-118, 131
Yiddish as common language. . 120
. . . . .123, 126, 153, 188

Printed in the United States
79284LV00002B/142